PREACHING
HEBREWS AND 1 PETER

PROCLAMATION:
Preaching the New Testament

Before the rise of historical criticism as the dominant mode of interpretation in the eighteenth century, biblical commentaries were written for the church with homiletical interests in mind. Since the Enlightenment, the critical commentary has largely excluded ecclesiastical and homiletical interests. In introducing the Meyer series in 1831, H. A. W. Meyer set the standard for subsequent commentaries, indicating that this commentary would exclude philosophical and ecclesiastical concerns and would concentrate on what the original authors meant in their own historical context.

This standard creates a challenge for preachers whose task is to bring a living word to listeners, most of whom do not come to church out of anti-quarian interests. Some commentaries have attempted to overcome the gap between the historical interests of the critical commentary and the homiletical concerns of the preacher by publishing parallel sections—one providing critical scholarship and the other offering guidance for preaching.

While biblical scholars specialize in a specific genre or book of Scripture, preachers are responsible for interpreting the entire canon over an extended time. As commentaries are increasingly complex, few preachers have the opportunity to mine the information and reflect an awareness of contemporary scholarship on each passage. Thus they face the challenge of merging the horizons between critical scholarship and a living word for the congregation.

In these volumes, scholar-preachers and preacher-scholars offer a guide for preachers, bringing the horizons of past and present together. The series is not a typical commentary, but a guide for preachers that offers the results of scholarship for the sake of preaching. Writers in this series will reflect an awareness of critical scholarship but will not focus on the details involved in a commentary. Rather, they will offer the fruits of critical scholarship reflected in explanations of sections of the biblical text. After a brief discussion of the major issues in a book—the central issues—each volume will be arranged by sections with an eye to what is useful for the sermon.

Authors in the Proclamation series will describe the major focus of each section, recognizing the place of the passage in the context of the book. Authors will look to the rhetorical impact of the text, asking "what does the text do?" Does it reassure the hearers? Does it lead them in worship and praise? Does it indict? Does it encourage? The Proclamation series will guide preachers in recognizing the essential rhetorical focus of the passage towards representing the impact of the text for today.

While preachers offer a living word for a specific situation, they also speak to larger cultural issues that face every congregation. Consequently, writers in this series may employ their knowledge of the ancient situation to suggest how the ancient word speaks across the centuries to parallel situations in our own time.

Accompanying the discussion writers may employ sermons, outlines, or other resources that further empower today's preachers in making the use of scholarship for the good of the church today.

Series Editors:

James W. Thompson is Scholar in Residence in the Graduate School of Theology at Abilene Christian University as well as the editor for Restoration Quarterly.

Jason A. Myers is Associate Professor of Biblical Studies at Greensboro College, Greensboro, NC.

Preaching

HEBREWS AND 1 PETER

த

James W. Thompson

CASCADE *Books* · Eugene, Oregon

PREACHING HEBREWS AND 1 PETER

Proclamation: Preaching the New Testament

Cascade Books
An Imprint of Wipf and Stock Publishers
199 W. 8th Ave., Suite 3
Eugene, OR 97401

www.wipfandstock.com

PAPERBACK ISBN: 978-1-6667-0529-4
HARDCOVER ISBN: 978-1-6667-0530-0
EBOOK ISBN: 978-1-6667-0531-7

Cataloguing-in-Publication data:

Names: Thompson, James W., author.

Title: Preaching Hebrews and 1 Peter / by James W. Thompson.

Description: Eugene, OR: Cascade Books, 2021 | Series: Proclamation: Preaching the New Testament | Includes bibliographical references.

Identifiers: ISBN 978-1-6667-0529-4 (paperback) | ISBN 978-1-6667-0530-0 (hardcover) | ISBN 978-1-6667-0531-7 (ebook)

Subjects: LCSH: Bible. Hebrews—Homiletical use. | Bible. Hebrews—Criticism, interpretation, etc. | Bible. Peter, 1st—Homiletical use. | Bible. Peter, 1st—Criticism, interpretation, etc. | Preaching.

Classification: BS2775.2 T56 2021 (print) | BS2775.2 (ebook)

11/09/21

CONTENTS

HEBREWS

A BRIEF INTRODUCTION
TO HEBREWS

SEMINARY STUDENTS ANXIOUSLY AWAITED their assignment from their homiletics professor that would be posted with each student's assigned text for the final sermon. The assignment was an exegesis of a particular text and a sermon demonstrating the relationship between critical exegesis and preaching. Students were anxious because some would be assigned familiar texts such as the prodigal son, while others would receive an obscure passage from 1 or 2 Chronicles or, "even worse, the Story of Balaam's ass." A crowd gathered as soon as the lists were posted. A student in his final semester was distressed with the passage assigned to him. "Darn it," he said. "I got a text from Hebrews. I really wanted a New Testament text."[1]

Preaching from Hebrews is a daunting task, even for those who are more familiar with this homily than this seminary student was. What preacher would not prefer to expound on the parables or stories about Jesus? Preachers are faced with their own unfamiliarity with the book as well as the unfamiliarity of their audience to this mysterious book. What we do remember are esoteric arguments, the mysterious figure of Melchizedek, the furnishings of the tabernacle, and the repeated claim that there is no repentance for those who fall away. Furthermore, we are faced with the anonymity of the author and our ignorance about the identity of the original audience. Who can preach this?

1. Jones, "Formed and Transformed by Scripture," 18.

3

Our first clue is to recognize the unique genre of this book. Its purpose is not to give esoteric arguments, although they are prominent in this homily, but to be a "word of exhortation," the term for a homily (cf. Acts 13:15). With its obscure references and the lengthy treatment of the Levitical cult, we might consider it a strange kind of sermon. It is a challenge to imagine how the original audience heard it as a word of exhortation and a greater challenge to imagine how it is a word of exhortation for us. That is, how is this book "sharper than any two-edged sword" for us?

Because of the series of comparisons declaring that Jesus is "better than" Old Testament people and institutions, interpreters have traditionally argued that the readers are tempted to return to Judaism and that the focus is that Christianity is better than Judaism. This interpretation is flawed for three reasons: 1) The author never indicates that the readers are tempted to return to Judaism; 2) it fails to acknowledge the frequent exhortations in the homily; and 3) comparisons of this kind were a common mode of argument known as *synkrisis*, according to the teachers of rhetoric. *Synkrisis* was a means of exalting someone by choosing a point of comparison that would be familiar to the audience.

The missing dimension in the traditional reading of Hebrews is the placement of the exhortations that appear intermittently throughout the book. Indeed, the unique aspect of the genre of Hebrews is that exhortations are like stitches between theological arguments (cf. 2:1–4; 3:7—4:11; 5:11–6:8; 10:19–39). That is, theological arguments lead to exhortation. The author encourages readers of the second generation (2:1–4; 10:32–34) who have "drooping hands and weak knees" (12:12). Some are abandoning the assembly (10:25), and the whole church is lacking in endurance (cf. 10:36–39; 12:1–11). The author is concerned that they will "drift away" (2:1) and "fall away from the living God" (3:12; cf. 6:4). The listeners suffer from the fatigue that is characteristic of most movements that suffer from declining enthusiasm. Thus Hebrews speaks to a church in need of renewal. The most basic question for the readers is: Is it worth it to be a Christian? We find our point of contact with the readers and listen for a word that speaks to us as well as to them. The decline and aging of the churches indicate that churches in the present also face decline in attendance and a generation that no longer sees the value of life in the Christian community. Consequently, every sermon on Hebrews should reflect a knowledge that the entire book is meant to encourage faint-hearted readers to maintain their commitment to Christ and the community. Even the most obscure parts are intended to answer the question: Is it worth it to be a Christian?

The Significance of the Structure of Hebrews for Preaching

The selection of the text requires a knowledge of the structure of Hebrews and the place of our passage within the sequence of the argument. Hebrews is divided into three parts. The central section has the bookends indicated below. The exhortation surrounding the arguments of Hebrews indicate that the theology and exhortation are deeply related.[2]

4:14–16	10:19–23
Therefore, having a great high priest	Therefore, having . . . a great priest
who has passed through the heavens,	. . . through the curtain . . .
Jesus, the Son of God,	by the blood of Jesus,
let us hold fast to the confession	let us hold fast the confession
let us draw near . . . with boldness	let us draw near with a true heart . . .

This *inclusio* results in a tripartite structure. Part 1 of Hebrews has an *inclusio* that is framed by the opening periodic sentence, focusing on the fact that God "has spoken in his son" (1:1), and the periodic sentence on God's word in 4:12–13. The bookends in part 2 (4:14—10:31) enclose the treatment of the high priest, the sanctuary, and the sacrifice, indicating that the exposition on the high priestly work of Christ builds the case for the exhortation to hold on to the Christian confession (4:14; 10:23). The final section (10:32—13:35) is composed primarily of exhortations that draw the consequences of the theological section and call for faithfulness. With the juxtaposition of the theological and paraenetic sections, the author shows that the center of gravity is in the exhortations. Thus the author of Hebrews demonstrates how theology serves preaching.

2. See Thompson, *Hebrews*, 15.

The Selection of Texts for Preaching

My task is not to offer a commentary explaining all of the nuances of the author's argument; preachers should consult the commentaries for the detailed analysis (see the recommended commentaries below). Since the author intersperses commentary with exhortation, with rare exceptions the texts chosen for preaching in Hebrews will include the relevant exhortations. If we do not include the exhortations, we should demonstrate the pastoral nature of each passage as a word for an exhausted church.

Since my task is not to write a commentary, we should find the center of gravity for each passage and focus on it. Thomas Long's recommendation of a focus and function statement is a useful exercise.[3] In reading our text, we want to be able to find the main idea and distinguish it from the supporting arguments. We focus on the decisive point in the section and leave our community with one major message. I recommend that the focus and function statements be followed by a plot or sketch prior to the full development of the sermon. The sketch should track the basic movement of the sermon.[4] In this book, I have followed David Buttrick's model of a sermon plot with a series of moves.[5]

The preacher should recognize the narrative quality of Hebrews in order to grasp the focus. The author addresses readers who are in the middle of a narrative that has a beginning and an end, and he writes to ensure the proper outcome. Similarly, we speak to communities that are in the middle of their own narrative, and our story intersects those of the first readers. Like the author of Hebrews, we preach to ensure the desired outcome of our listeners.

As Fred Craddock has argued,[6] unity and movement are the primary characteristics of the effective sermon. Therefore, the sequence of thought in the sketch should, like any good narrative, have a beginning, a middle, and an end. Consequently, the sketch should move toward a conclusion.

Interpreting the text for preaching also requires reflection on how the text speaks to the congregation today. In Hebrews, for example, our congregation can identify with the struggles of the first readers. Churches

---

3. Long, *Witness of Preaching*, 78–91.

4. See Buttrick, *Homiletic*, 37–79, 313–18, for the sermon sketch as the plot for the sermon.

5. Buttrick, *Homiletic*, 23–36.

6. Craddock, *Preaching*, 153; cf. Craddock, *As One without Authority*, 51–76.

facing the challenges of renewal today will hear the solution offered by the author of Hebrews in a similar situation at the end of the first century. Just as the author contemporized ancient texts to address his audience, the preachers continue demonstrating the power of ancient words in addressing our own situation. While preachers do not go into detail in describing the situation of the ancient readers, their sermons reflect an awareness of the situation that evoked the message of Hebrews as they address a comparable situation in our own time.

Chapter 1

HEARING GOD'S VOICE

Hebrews 1:1—4:13

1:1–4. Exegetical Reflections.

HEBREWS 1:1–4 IS OVERWHELMING in its power. The preacher should be attentive not only to what is said, but how the author said it. He uses poetry (it is one sentence in Greek), intended to affect both the mind and the emotions as he introduces the major themes of the book: God has spoken (1:1–2; cf. 12:25); the Christ event is God's oath (cf. 6:13–20); Jesus has made purification for sins (1:3; cf. 7:1–10:18); Jesus is "better than" (1:4; 6:9; 7:7, 19; 8:6; 10:34; 12:24); Jesus is at God's right hand (1:4; 8:10; 10:12).

The author recognizes the importance of opening words. Like the ancient rhetorical theorists, he recognizes that the introduction should a) introduce the topic and b) make the audience favorably disposed. The author does not mention the most pressing issue facing the audience, but he writes with keen awareness of the problems that the listeners face. The passage answers the question: Is it worth it to be a Christian? The poetry suggests a resounding "yes." With its powerful poetic introduction, it indicates that the author is himself overwhelmed by the message.

Ancient teachers of rhetoric spoke of the argument from ethos as one of the major modes of argumentation. Here the rhetorical power suggests the author's own engagement with the subject. Effective preaching on this passage will demonstrate the preacher's own engagement with the text and encourage listeners to experience its power.

Interpretation involves identifying the main clause and its relationship to supporting clauses. In the opening sentence, "God, who has spoken to our ancestors in many and various ways, has spoken in these last days in a Son," the main clause is "God has spoken in these last days in a Son." The passage then follows with dependent clauses celebrating the greatness of the Son, who was present at the creation and now reigns above all powers. As the remainder of the letter indicates, God has spoken in the Christ event—the incarnation, death, and exaltation of Christ. The description of the preexistence ("through whom he made the worlds," "radiance of his glory," "exact representation of his being"), the incarnation and death ("having made purification for sins"), and the exaltation of Christ ("he sat at the right hand of the majesty") is reminiscent of other poetic summaries of the entire story of Christ (cf. Phil 2:6–11). The contrast between "in many and various ways" and "in these last days" indicates the finality of Jesus Christ, who is not one option among many. "Greater than the angels," like the numerous other comparisons in Hebrews, also indicates that Christ is not one option of many.

The author describes the greatness of Christ, employing the first of many comparisons in the homily, the device known as *synkrisis* by the teachers of rhetoric, who maintained that comparison is the means for demonstrating the greatness of a person. The comparisons in Hebrews do not reflect the audience's allegiance to the objects of comparison (angels, the Levitical system, Mount Sinai), but their basic familiarity with these topics. If the author had spoken in a different era, he probably would have used other objects of comparison.

Engaging the conversation between the ancient text and the audience, the author reminds the readers of the key to renewal, which does not lie in novel ideas or strategies but in a recognition of the message that called them into being. He returns to the community's basic confession that had called it into existence, appealing to what they have already affirmed. We observe that God has spoken to "us"—the exhausted community that exists as a small minority in a hostile society. We have a powerful message that the world does not know.

The sermon is the occasion for preachers to demonstrate their own ethos. Just as the author appears to still be awed by the message, preachers should demonstrate their own commitment to the church's confession. Preachers may recall how they themselves return to God's ultimate word as the orienting factor in their own lives. Repetition of the passage throughout the sermon will offer the opportunity for the community to reclaim its own orientation.

In an attempt to establish anticipation, I have sketched the movement from the problem to the resolution. The focus statement is frequently the conclusion of the sermon, and the earlier moves are intended to lead the reader toward the conclusion.

Sermon Focus: In our discouragement, when we are a declining insignificant minority, what do we need to hear? The message that called us together at the beginning: God has spoken the ultimate word in the Son. [Note: I recommend that we recite the words at the beginning and end of the sermon, hoping to do what the text does: express the power of the message and experience the text.]

Sermon Function: To awaken the discouraged congregation to a renewed recognition of the grandeur of the faith as the only remedy for their situation.

Sermon Sketch: Hearing God's Ultimate Word

Reading of Heb 1:1–4. Every preacher, every storyteller, every dramatist knows the importance of opening words. I am reminded of Frederick Buechner's description of the preacher's challenge. It may also be my own. According to Frederick Buechner,

> the preacher pulls the little cord that turns on the lectern light and deals out his note cards like a riverboat gambler. The stakes have never been higher. Two minutes from now he may have lost his listeners completely to their own thoughts, but at this minute he has them in the palm of his hand. The silence in the shabby church is deafening because everybody is listening to it. Everybody is listening including even himself. Everybody knows the kind of things he has told them before and not told them, but who knows what this time, out of the silence, he will tell them?[1]

The challenge of the author of Hebrews is our common challenge. What do you say to those who almost did not come? To those who have heard the message many times before? That was the challenge then, and it is the challenge now.

---

1. Buechner, *Telling the Truth*, 33.

1. Will the church survive? The signs in the western world do not look good. We struggle with the aging of the church, the loss of a generation, and even the hostility to organized religion. Of course, the question of the survival of the church is as old as the late first century, when the author of Hebrews wrote to a second-generation church. People were dropping out of church then. The author was faced with the dilemma that we face now: How do we ensure the growth—or even the survival—of the church? I suggest that the author of Hebrews has much to say to us, for he provides an insight as he faces a church that was asking the question we are asking.

2. We are not lacking in recommendations and strategies for the renewal of the church: change the worship style, offer a more relevant message, rearrange the furniture. The literature on church renewal is abundant—and often superficial. Is there not a deeper problem?

3. The author of Hebrews gives the answer (read Heb 1:1–4): to hear once more and to celebrate the words that brought us to faith in the first place. Indeed, the words are so powerful that the author has put it into poetry because he is still moved by the message: Jesus Christ is God's final word. God has spoken in a Son, God's own image, who "made purification for sins" on earth and now reigns with God." There is no message like it.

4. What is the answer for an exhausted church? Not a superficial response, but a reaffirmation of the message that brought us into the family of God at the beginning. In the 1960s sociologist Peter Berger was asked if Christianity would survive in the twenty-first century. He replied that it would probably be different, perhaps smaller. Some would not survive. But those who had a clear message that Christ was God's ultimate word would survive. Indeed, the preservation of the book of Hebrews and the continuing survival of the church through the centuries is evidence of the power of the word that "God has spoken in a Son."

1:1—2:4. Exegetical Reflections.

This lengthy section also forms an appropriate unit. The preacher may incorporate 1:1–4 into the longer passage, shifting the focus primarily to

1:1–14 and 2:1–4. The series of Scripture citations in 1:5–14 simply confirms what is said in 1:1–4 and should not be the focus. The declaration in chapter 1 now leads to the exhortation in 2:1–4. Using the nautical image of a people without an anchor, the author addresses the issue facing the readers for the first time, expressing concern that the readers may "drift away." To do so would be to "neglect the great salvation" (2:4).

In 1:1–4 the author says, "God has spoken to us," and 2:1–4 says that "it is necessary to pay attention to what we have heard" (2:1), which was "spoken by the Lord and confirmed to us by those who heard him" (2:3). This passage demonstrates the significance of the fact that the exalted Christ is "greater than angels" (1:4), for this is the "great salvation" (2:4). The author continues the comparison to two different words—the one delivered by angels (2:2) and the one spoken by the Lord. That is, the greater the message, the more the consequences for not paying attention. We should pay attention to what the Lord has spoken because the consequences are severe (see this theme repeated in 12:25–29). The author goes on later to describe the Israelites who did not endure and thus missed out on the promised land (3:7–19). Thus believers are not casual in listening to God's word, even if they have heard it many times already.

Sermon Focus: We are surrounded by words in every direction, so much so that we ignore them—empty promises by politicians, the advertiser's pitch, constant chatter of the media. But God has spoken to us in a voice like none other, and God demands attention as we hear his voice. God's word calls for a response.

Sermon Function: To awaken the listeners to the need for paying attention to what we have heard, recognizing the consequences for not listening to the ultimate word.

Sermon Sketch on Heb 1:1—2:4: Pay Attention to the Words that Matter

Introduction. We are inundated by words. We cannot stand the silence. Words on the radio, the words on television constantly blaring "breaking news," words on the internet, words on the robocalls that inundate us. With so many words, we learn to filter out the many messages. What if we are so immersed in "news" that we easily miss words that are a matter of life and death?

1. We may, as the author of Hebrews suggests, "drift away" from the word that God has spoken. After all, we have heard it before, countless times. It becomes so familiar that we tune it out.

2. But this word has changed our lives: God has spoken God's ultimate word (1:1–2; 2:1–2), and God has spoken *to us* a word that is not like other words. This is the word that we first accepted when we became believers.

3. The ultimate word summons listeners—even those who have heard the message before—to "pay attention," recognizing that this is the "great salvation."

4. "To neglect the great salvation" is to be accountable before God's judgment ("how shall we escape?"). God's ultimate word requires a response. As the author of Hebrews indicates, there are those who "died in faith," but there were others who missed out on the great salvation. There is a time to hear, with the author of Hebrews, that God is the one to whom we give an account, that God is a consuming fire, that it is a fearful thing to fall into the hands of the living God. Uncomfortable words, to be sure. It is a reminder that the loving God has spoken, that his word is to be taken seriously.

2:5–18. Exegetical Reflections.

This passage appears at first to be a continuation of the claim that Christ is higher than the angels; the passage cited (Ps 8) continues the series of Scripture citations from chapter 1. The author has taken Ps 8, which originally spoke of the place of humankind in the universe, and applied it to Christ. In the phrase, "you have made him a little while lower than the angels" (the Hebrew of the Psalm says "a little lower than the elohim/ divine beings"), the author refers to the incarnation. "Crowned with glory and honor" (2:7) and "you have put all things under his feet" (2:8) refer to the exaltation of Christ, the consistent theme of Hebrews. The key to the interpretation of 2:5–18 is the phrase in 2:8c, "But we do not see all things in subjection to him." This is probably the reaction of the readers to the lofty words about the triumph of Christ: Yes, but we do not see it. The remainder of the passage (2:10–18) is an answer to that objection. What we see is the one who reached the exalted status only through the path of suffering the same temptations the readers now experience. That is, the sufferings now experienced are the prelude to the end; Jesus is the "pioneer" (2:10) on that path.

The author consistently employs the image of a trek through the wilderness toward the heavenly homeland for the Christian life. This trek is a corporate reality, as Ernst Käsemann demonstrated in the classic *The Wandering People of God*. The pioneer (*archēgos*) opens the way for others to follow (other translations have "author" or "leader"); the author uses a similar image of "forerunner" in 6:20. The image suggests that the pioneer has led the way through uncharted territory. In this instance, the pioneer reached the "power and glory" only through the path of suffering. The passage indicates his total solidarity with the community; they have "one Father" (2:11); thus they are brothers and sisters (2:12–13), sharing flesh and blood (2:14). The one who has been crowned with glory and honor once stood where the listeners stand. He has experienced the same temptations that the readers are now facing (2:17).

Interpreters have often observed the low-high Christology of Hebrews. No epistle emphasizes the full humanity of Jesus as much as Hebrews (cf. 4:15; 5:7–10), and no book emphasizes the exaltation as thoroughly as Hebrews. Heb 2:5–18 speaks of the humanity of Jesus and his solidarity with believers in 2:10–18. The author's interest is not, however, in an abstract teaching on Christology. His focus is totally pastoral. The one who was fully human—"like his brothers in every respect" (2:17) —has faced the trials that the community now faces. The pioneer is the one who leads the way for others to follow. The pioneer entered into glory only through the path of suffering. Thus the current suffering of the believers—their marginalization, discouragement, and hostility from neighbors—is not merely a misfortune but is the necessary precondition in which they follow the pioneer to triumph.

Sermon Focus: Believers doubt if it is worthwhile to be a Christian because they see no victories. As the author of Hebrews concedes, "We do not see all things in subjection to him." However, we see the one who shared all our temptations, knowing that his sufferings led to victory.

Sermon Function: To encourage the community in its time of testing to remain steadfast, knowing that Christ the pioneer has faced the same temptations.

Sermon Sketch on 2:5–18: Following Jesus through the Wilderness

Introduction: Praise songs celebrating victory can be stirring for worshipers. Many of the great hymns lift our spirits. We recall the stirring words at the opening of Hebrews, and we hear the words of Ps 8, which are cited by the author of Hebrews, who sees Jesus "crowned with glory and honor." We have countless praise songs that declare "victory in Jesus."

1. But then we face reality: As the author of Hebrews says, "we do not see" the triumph. What we celebrate in song does not correspond to our own struggles. It has always been that way. We share that experience with the first readers of Hebrews. The author of Hebrews describes a people on a journey to the promised land as they face discouragement and exhaustion. They cannot see the promised land, the victory. We can identify with them, for we too experience the wilderness in our own faith.

2. "We do not see" the victory, but "we see Jesus," the pioneer who shared our struggle and temptation. "We do not see" a remote victor, but one who has total solidarity with the community. Hebrews employs a vivid image for the people on the journey. Ahead of them is the pioneer (*archēgos*) who has blazed the trail and opened the way and ultimately was "crowned with glory and honor." Only through suffering did he become victorious.

3. Only one who has shared our experience can understand and help. The one who was tempted stands by believers in their struggles—even in their doubts. And then he was victorious. "Victory in Jesus" took place only through the path of hardship and suffering.

3:1–6. Exegetical Reflections.

Hebrews is a series of comparisons. This comparison of Christ with Moses is a reprise of the earlier comparison of Christ with the angels; that is, Christ is a son rather than a servant in the house (3:5–6), just as Christ is a Son, while angels are servants (1:14). As with all the comparisons, this is the basis for the pastoral affirmation and exhortation. "*We* are *his* house" recalls the earlier "God has spoken to *us*" (1:2). *We* do not belong to an ordinary house (house is the common biblical word for family), but to the house/family of the one who has triumphed. That is, the minority community should not give up; it has a special place in God's plan as God's house. "If we hold firmly" is the exhortation, indicating the temptation of the community to let go of its faith. The author likes verbs for "holding firmly" or grasping (cf. 3:14; 6:18; 10:23). It suggests the need for an intense response to God's gift with all our energy so that the gift will not slip away.

The dominant image of the passage is that of family. The author has already indicated the family solidarity between Christ and believers (2:12–13) and now focuses on God's house. The preacher may want to focus on this image, indicating that the marginalized people—even those who have negative experiences with family—belong to God's family.

Sermon Focus: God has given believers an extraordinary privilege—to be members of the household of the Son of God. Even if we are marginalized by society, "we are *his* house." But our task is to "hold on" in the worst of circumstances, in the midst of discouragement and the desire to give up.

Sermon Function: To demonstrate that while the community is marginalized by society, it has a special place in God's family, but this privilege must be held tightly lest it slip away.

Sermon Sketch: Family Values

Introduction: Family values mean different things to different people. For some, "there is no place like home," while for others it is the place of acrimony and dysfunction. Believers in the ancient world frequently lost the security of home because of their commitment to this new religion, leaving them homeless. In the present climate of our culture, some are literally homeless and others are metaphorically homeless. The first readers of Hebrews were, in a sense, homeless. Their marginalization led to an identity crisis.

Believers today find themselves marginalized—homeless—in the larger culture. As Hebrews indicates, this homelessness leads to discouragement and temptations to withdraw from the fellowship of believers.

1. We, the community of faith, are his house, a place for homeless people. For all who have lost the security of family, God has provided a new family. For all who have never enjoyed the security of the physical family, God has provided the church. Many of us have been separated from our physical families by distance, but we have found a family among God's people.

2. But we are not only a family. We are *his* house. We have a place to belong in the family of the one who gave himself and then triumphed. As

Hebrews indicates, Jesus Christ is the faithful Son in God's house. This is no ordinary house. I recall Fred Craddock's story of the little boy who lived alone with his mother. As a poor person on the wrong side of the tracks with no father, he and his mother did not dare enter a church where they would face judgmental eyes. One day, however, the young boy gained the courage to visit the little church, all the while trying not to be noticed. The minister, however, noticed the young boy and asked, "Whose son are you?" Then the minister replied, "Oh, I know. You are God's child."

3. *"If we hold firmly."* In trying circumstances our task is to respond to God's gift with determination, knowing that we live in hope of reaching the destination.

3:7—4:11 (or 3:7—4:13). Exegetical Reflections.

A consistent image throughout Hebrews is that of the people on the way. Ernst Käsemann's classic book on Hebrews is entitled *The Wandering People of God*. This image is an appropriate reminder that the readers belong to a minority group that is, in a sense, homeless. This midrash on Ps 95:7–11 reinforces the "if" clause in 3:6 (repeated in 3:14) and continues to presuppose the story of Moses. The Psalm recalls the days in Israel's rebellion in the wilderness (Exod 17:7; Num 14:20–23); the psalmist urges his people not to harden their hearts, as the wilderness generation had done. Like the psalmist, the author applies that story to a later generation. The author has a special interest in the divine oath, "They shall never enter my rest" (Heb 3:11). The ancient words of the psalmist are now speaking to the church as the voice of the Holy Spirit now speaks to his own listeners (Heb 3:7). He recalls the words of God, quoted in the Psalm, "I swore in my wrath, they shall not enter my rest" (Heb 3:11).

As the author's comments indicate, the possibility of entering God's rest remains a possibility for his listeners, but the listeners are in danger of forfeiting it. He never acknowledges that Israel actually entered into the promised land but concludes that Israel did not enter the promised rest because of their unbelief (3:19), their failure to endure in difficult circumstances. The rest that the author mentions is no longer Canaan, however, but the heavenly homeland.

The negative example of Israel in 3:7—4:11 stands in contrast to the positive examples in chapter 11. While Israel did not enter God's rest because of its unbelief (*apistia*, 3:12, 19), the heroes of faith lived "by faith" (*pistis*, ch. 11). Neither in the negative example (3:7—4:11) nor the positive example of faithfulness (ch. 11) did the patriarchs enter the promised land. However, the faithful heroes "died in faith, not having received the promise" (11:13), but they endured as long as they lived.

The passage is divided into two parts (three parts if we include 4:12–13). In the first part (3:7–19), after quoting Ps 95:7–11, the author urges the people to respond to the "today" of the Psalm, challenges them to encourage one another each day (3:12–13), and warns of the consequences of failure (3:16–19), not even conceding that anyone entered the promised land. In the second part (4:1–11), the author maintains that, while Israel failed to enter the promised land, the way stands open ("God's rest") for those who are faithful. Here the author has redefined "rest," which is no longer the earthly Canaan, but the heavenly world. [Note all the hymns that evoke the image of the promised land as heaven.] By equating two Scriptures that contain the word "rest" (Ps 95:11; Gen 2:2) the author concludes that "God's rest" on the seventh day (Gen 2:2) is the equivalent to the "rest" described in the Psalm. Thus he concludes that Israel did not enter that rest but that there remains "a sabbath (rest) for the people of God" (4:9). And he urges the readers to enter God's rest.

The third part (4:12–13) is a reflection on the word of God, which is "sharper than any two-edged sword." While the passage appears to stand alone, as the paragraphing in the NRSV suggests, it is an appropriate conclusion to the midrash on 3:7–11. The "word of God" in 4:12 recalls the introductory statement that "God has Spoken in the Son" (1:2), a message that was also "spoken by the Lord" (2:3). It also recalls God's oath, "They shall never enter my rest" (3:11) and the irrevocability of that oath, which announces both salvation and punishment (cf. 4:1). That word is known to the community through Scripture (3:7—4:11).

The imagery of the sword dominates the author's reflections, indicating that the word of God is an instrument of judgment, piercing the innermost parts of the person. As God's oath to Israel indicates, those who hear God's voice mediated in Scripture are confronted by the God who is the "judge of all" (cf. 12:23). The surgical capabilities of the word now confront the community that is faced with a decision about its response.

The preacher might choose all of 3:7—4:13 as a sermon text. When we read Scripture, we find ourselves in the characters. Scripture is "living and active" when we see ourselves in the story. That is, we see that, like the Israelites, we need to pay attention or miss out on the promised land. We find hope in the fact that "there remains a Sabbath rest for the people of God." The sermon can be a message of both warning and hope.

The first part of the passage (3:7-19) is also an appropriate unit for preaching. We note the bookends that begin with the author's comments on the passage: "Beware lest there be in any one of you an evil heart of unfaithfulness" (*apistia*) in 3:12 and "we see that they were not able to enter because of unfaithfulness" (*apistia*) in 3:19. *Apistia* is the negative of *pistis* (faith), the theme of Heb 11. As Heb 10:36–39 and 12:1–11 indicate, faith is closely associated with endurance. Hence faith is not merely believing that something is true; it is *faithfulness* in difficult circumstances.

Preaching from 3:7-19 requires that we distinguish between the main idea and the supporting argument. The main idea is present in the two imperatives in 3:12-13: "Beware lest there be in any of you. . ." and "encourage each other every day," which is followed by the supporting argument (3:14-19). Both imperatives indicate the corporate nature of the community's journey, as the phrase "lest there be any of you" indicates. The argument for the exhortation is a) "we are partakers of Christ, if we hold firmly" (3:14) and the negative example of Israel (3:15-19). As "anyone of you" (3:12) and "each other" (3:13) indicate, the passage is a call for community solidarity as a means for the whole community to remain faithful.

Undoubtedly the readers of Hebrews were facing a crisis of faithfulness. The words of Heb 2:8c, "But we do not see everything in subjection to him," probably reflect the crisis of the readers. It is one thing to claim the victory of Jesus Christ; it is quite another to see the evidence of it. Heb 3:12-19 speaks to that crisis, warning of the possibility of missing out on the inheritance that God has promised to the faithful.

Sermon Focus (3:12-19): Faced with our own discouragement as we journey, we maintain our faithfulness in solidarity with others, encouraging each other each day; the negative example of our ancestors is a warning to us.

Sermon Function: To encourage communal solidarity, describing our common responsibility to care for all, recalling the lessons from Israel's unfaithfulness in the wilderness.

Sermon Sketch (3:7-19): *A Trek through the Wilderness*

I understand that the term *trek* entered the English language from the Dutch Afrikaans, recalling the arduous journey of the Boers in 1835 from British rule in the coastal cape of South Africa to a homeland in the north and east. It has come to mean an arduous task that we voluntarily take—the Appalachian Trail, Hadrian's Wall, a path in the Alps. It is the challenge only for those who are physically strong.

1. As the author of Hebrews suggests, Christian existence is a trek through the wilderness, not a stroll in the park. Even for the physically fit, it is an endurance test, the experience of those who are at present homeless in the culture. It is a long journey. We hope to reach our destination, but we do not see it.

2. As we consider our own experience in a post-Christian culture, we learn from ancestors who faced the same temptations. Israel wandered in the wilderness in a test of faithfulness. They complained about the food and the water, even wishing that they could return to Egypt, and God said, "They will never enter my rest." As the author of Hebrews tells the story, Israel failed because of its failure to endure—its *unfaithfulness*. It was a warning to his own community and a warning to us, for our faithfulness is also tested in unpleasant circumstances.

3. But this trek involves the whole community, and it is composed of many who are not physically (or spiritually) fit. We do not look out only for own conditioning on the trek, but we ensure that no one is left behind. Some are aged and infirm; others become discouraged and wish to abandon the trek. Because we reach our destination only in solidarity with each other, we "encourage one another" and see that "no one" is left behind.

4. Near the end of the homily, the author recalls the heroes who never gave up; they were examples of *pistis*—faithfulness—which the author equates with endurance in the midst of disappointment and suffering. But the wilderness generation failed because of *apistia*—unfaithfulness, and the whole community missed out.

5. The church faces exhaustion on its own trek. Can we learn from Israel that this is a corporate trek and that we survive only when we see that no one is left behind.

The second part of the passage (4:1–11) is also an appropriate unit for preaching. It begins with an exhortation that paraphrases the exhortation in 3:12–13: "Let us take care that none of you should seem to have failed to enter [God's] rest." Once more "[not] any of you" (NRSV "none of you") points to communal solidarity. The supporting arguments appear in 4:2–11 (note "for indeed" in 4:2 and "for" in 4:3). In the first argument (4:2), the author indicates that the readers received the same good news that Israel received but that Israel failed because of lack of faith (cf. 3:19). In the second argument (4:3–11), the author indicates that, although Israel did not enter the promised land, the promise still remains available for the believing community. As the argument about God's rest indicates (4:4), the "rest" is no longer Canaan but heaven. One may compare the numerous references to the promise in Hebrews (cf. 6:12; 11:13, 17).

While 3:7–19 is a warning not to repeat Israel's example, 4:1–11 is an encouragement to weary listeners that the goal still lies ahead. What motivates them is the certainty of the promise. The author does not envision the march to the promised land as an individual matter, for the church is on the journey together.

The main point of 4:1–11 may be observed in the bookends that frame the passage. The "let us passages" in 4:1, 11 indicate the center of gravity of the passage. It is an exhortation to enter God's rest, which has already been identified as the heavenly promised land. The remainder of the passage is the argument that the rest is still available for believers. The parallel passages in 4:3, 9 are assurances that the divine promise is still available for believers. This fact is the basis for the exhortations in 4:1, 11. The passage is a reminder that we live in hope even if present circumstances are difficult. It is also a reminder that the church is the continuation of ancient Israel and still has the possibility of completing the journey although its predecessors did not reach the goal.

Sermon Focus (4:1–11). The exhausted community lives in hope that it will complete the journey that other generations failed to complete.

Sermon Function: To urge the exhausted community to complete the journey because it lives in hope for the future provided by God.

Sermon Sketch: The Hope That Sustains Us

Introduction: What sustains people in dire circumstances is the hope for the future. What sustains the distance runner is the finish line. What sustains people on a trek is the prospect of reaching the goal.

1. The absence of hope is characteristic of our society. What will happen after the pandemic? What will be the effects of global warming? Will we face economic collapse? We are inundated by scenarios that end in disaster. The result is a society that lives for the moment, enjoying the pleasure of the moment.

2. But the church sees the future that God has prepared. Believers are a counterculture of hope. This hope for entering God's rest sustains believers in difficult times and differentiates the community from the hopelessness of society.

3. "Let us enter the rest," says the author of Hebrews. We continue to be sustained by hope, knowing what God has done in the past.

4:12–13. Exegetical Reflections.

In the NRSV and NIV, 4:12–13 is printed as a separate paragraph, suggesting that the statement about the word of God is a separate thought, a stitch between the example of Israel in 3:7—4:11 and the introduction of the high priestly work of Christ beginning in 4:14. As "indeed" (NRSV; Greek *gar*) in 4:12 indicates, the passage is the conclusion to the preceding section. The "word of God" here is a reference to God's oath, "They shall never enter my rest" (3:11). A major theme of Hebrews is that "God has spoken to us" (1:1; cf. 2:1–4) and is speaking to us today (12:25). While the author is not, strictly speaking, talking about the Bible, the Bible is the record of God's speech. God's word is an oath that expresses both the consequences of our failure to endure (2:1–4; 3:11) and the promise that God gives for entering the promised land (cf. 11:13–16). God's word is thus a voice of warning and hope. That it is "living and active" recalls the voice of Scripture that speaks to us "today." (4:7). While God's oath is a promise of the future hope (cf. Isa. 55), a "word that does not come back empty" (Isa. 55:11), it is also a word of judgment. The image of the two-edged sword that pierces between soul and spirit, joints and marrow suggests the role of Scripture that confronts us with our own failure and stands in judgment on us. The community reads Scripture, not only to find support, but to be confronted with the God who stands in judgment.

Sermon Focus: 4:12–13

In the history of Christianity, the Bible has often been used as a "sword" to confirm our own views and to combat alternative views. The Bible also confronts us with our failings and exposes our own shortcomings.

Sermon Function: To encourage our community to see itself in the story of Israel's unfaithfulness and to see that the Bible does surgery on us.

Sermon Sketch: The Word of God Is Living and Active

Introduction: The Bible is a classic, the perennial bestseller. But like most of the great classics, it is admired more than it is read. I recall hearing someone say, "I have always regarded the Bible the way I regard Shakespeare: I concede that it is good and let it go at that." The description of the contents of the Bible as "living and active" does not correspond to our own experience. Perhaps it is because we have given it that black cover and divided it into chapters and verses. Or perhaps it has functioned as a reference or law book—not something we actually read. For many of us, it has functioned as a weapon to use in an argument. In fact, many people refer to the Bible as a sword. I assume this means that it is a sword to be used on others.

1. The author of Hebrews invites his readers to engage in biblical interpretation of Israel's experience in the wilderness, declaring that this story is "living and active." The readers will see themselves in the ancient story of Israel in the wilderness. According to one way of telling the story, this is the account of God's promise of the land, a moment leading to conquest. We naturally think of Israel's story as our story, and we identify with them.

2. Most of us like stories because we cannot resist identifying with the characters in the story; most frequently we identify with the good guys and their stories of heroism and triumph. Perhaps we read the Bible in the same way.

3. However, this is a story of unfaithfulness. Do we see ourselves in the story? We are not Moses leading the way; we find ourselves in Israel with all its transgressions.

4. We find that "the word of God is living and active, sharper than any two-edged sword." It does surgery on us as we identify with Israel's unfaithfulness. My former teacher, James Sanders, used to say, "Whenever you read the Bible and it makes you self-righteous, you misunderstood it."

Chapter 2

DRAWING NEAR TO
THE SANCTUARY

Hebrews 4:14—10:31

The Central Section of Hebrews (4:14—10:31)

As we observed in the introduction, the central section of Hebrews is determined by the *inclusio* that frames 4:14—10:31. Both passages have the form that is typical of Hebrews, "Since we have . . . let us." What "we have" is a great high priest" (4:14; 10:21) who is sympathetic with our weaknesses (4:15) and who "in every respect has been tested as we are" (4:15), and "confidence to enter the sanctuary by the blood of Christ" (10:19). What we *have* is the basis for the exhortation "let us." Therefore "let us hold firmly" (4:14; 10:23), "draw near" (4:16; 10:22), [1] and "provoke one another to love and good deeds" (10:24). These bookends provide the context for reading the dense argument about the high priest, the sanctuary, and the sacrifice in the central section of Hebrews. Preaching on these texts should always assume that the argument leads to the exhortation, "Let us." Consequently, the choice of the text should be determined by the recognition that the argument is a pastoral word.

---

1. An additional exhortation appears in 10:24, let us "consider to stir one another up to love and good works."

4:14—5:10. Exegetical Reflections.

The central section of Hebrews (4:14—10:31) focuses on the greater high priest, greater sacrifice, and greater sanctuary. The subject of the high priest is introduced in 4:14—5:10, an appropriate text for preaching. The preacher's task is not to explain the passage or take it apart but to see this as a "word of encouragement." The focal point should be on the two "let us" (hortatory subjunctive) passages: "Let us hold fast the confession" (4:14) and "let us draw near," both of which are major themes in Hebrews. The verb "hold firmly" (*kratōmen*) connotes the maintaining of a strong grip that is in danger of slipping away; the author uses the same verb in 6:18 and the synonymous verb *katechein* in 3:6, 14; 10:23. "Let us hold fast" is a recurring theme in the homily, reflecting the danger that the readers will let go of their confession. To "draw near" (NRSV "approach") is the task of priests in the tabernacle. Believers now "draw near" (*proserchesthai* in worship, 4:16; 7:25; 10:1; 10:22; 12:18, 22). The description of the high priest in 4:15 and 5:1–10 is the basis for the exhortations in 4:14–16. The focus of the description is the humanity of Christ, which the author develops with the description of the high priest. The qualifications for priesthood, given in 5:1–4, are not actually derived from Scripture, which says nothing about the necessity that the high priest "deal gently" (*metriopathein*) with the ignorant and the wayward. *Metriopathein*, literally "to moderate the passions," is contrasted to "be sympathetic" (*sympathein*, 4:15). Thus the author compares the human Jesus, who demonstrated sympathy (*sympathein*), with the high priest, who moderated the passions (*metriopathein*). *Sympathein* meant "to feel the pain of another." The term was used for God's sympathy for humans (4 Macc. 5:25) and for a mother's care for her children (4 Macc. 14:13, 14, 18). The author offers a vivid portrayal of the total involvement of Jesus in the temptations that now face the community (5:7–10). "In the days of his flesh, Jesus offered up prayers and supplications, with loud cries and tears, to the one who could save him from death" (5:7), and "he learned obedience from what he suffered" (5:8). The preacher does not need to answer the quandaries of this passage (i.e., in what sense was "he heard" when he prayed to the one who could save him from death?). The passage explains why believers can "hold fast" and "draw near," that is, because Jesus Christ has both shared their temptations (4:15; 5:7–8) and triumphed over them. Thus he "opened the way" for them to draw near.

The passage indicates that the one who shared our sufferings ultimately triumphed. Because Jesus was exalted and designated Son and high priest (5:5), he has become the source of eternal salvation (5:9). The readers can look beyond their present sufferings that Jesus has shared with them to the ultimate triumph. Once more the image of "pioneer" (2:10) lies in the background. In his full humanity, with all its sufferings, Jesus leads the way to ultimate triumph.

The preacher's task is to communicate the pastoral and rhetorical point of the passage rather than speculate about all the temptations Jesus faced. The temptations are not those suggested in *The Last Temptation of Christ* but those experienced by an exhausted community. The main ideas presented are the exhortations, "let us hold the confession firmly" (4:14) and "let us draw near with confidence." The reason that we can "hold firmly" and "draw near" is that our forerunner has total sympathy with us, having shared our temptations, and is victorious.

Sermon Focus: To preach the text it is not necessarily to follow its sequence but to find its center of gravity. That is, in our temptations to give up, we can be encouraged that Jesus shared the very temptations that the believers now face, opening the way to triumph.

Function: To urge listeners to hold firmly—not to lose their grip—and to approach God in worship because Jesus shared their struggle and triumphed.

Sermon Sketch: Overcoming Temptation

The Psalmist says, "But as for me, my feet had almost stumbled; my steps had nearly slipped" (Ps 73:2). It is the common experience of the faithful. Our expectations for peace and tranquility in the faith face reality. It was that way with the readers of Hebrews, and it is that way for us as we face disappointments. While the Psalmist says, "my steps had nearly slipped," the author of Hebrews speaks consistently of holding firmly. It is the encouragement for people who are about to lose their grip. It is a perennial problem.

1. We remember that the faith began with "loud cries and tears" from the one whom we now serve. Consequently, he is sympathetic with us—not sympathetic in the superficial way with which we commonly offer sympathy—when we are about to lose our grip. In the true sense of sympathy as "feeling with," he knows our pain. His temptations were our temptations—the sense of powerlessness.

2. But his "loud cries and tears" were not the end of the story, for he is the high priest who has "passed through the heavens" (4:14).

3. Because he has experience all our temptations, he helps in time of need (4:16). We may be powerless, but the one who has triumphed over the temptations is the source of our salvation. We can "hold firmly to our confession" and "draw near to him in worship" because we follow the one who proceeded from all human temptations to ultimate victory.

5:11—6:12. Exegetical Reflections.

This section interrupts the description of the priest and sacrifice with an exhortation. It has bookends formed by the word "dull" (nōthroi): "dull of hearing" in 5:11 and "so that you will not be dull" (NRSV "sluggish") in 6:12. The passage moves from indictment (5:11–14) to a warning explaining the consequences of falling away (6:1–8) to reassuring words (6:9–12). The indictment (5:11–14) demonstrates the intellectual nature of Christianity; remaining steadfast means growing in knowledge. Indeed, while the author has a message that is "hard to explain" (5:11), he proceeds in 7:1—10:18 to present that message. "Dull of hearing" was a common expression for mental obtuseness. "Milk" and "meat" were common images in educational theory, according to which one proceeded from one to another. The passage suggests the intellectual dimension of Christianity. Christian growth is not only a matter of the heart but also of the mind. Solid food is the advanced teaching that is required for ethical discernment (5:14). One requisite for the community's survival, therefore, is for the entire church to develop a deepening understanding of the Christian faith. The task of theology is not only for professionals but also for the entire community.

The warning in 6:1–8 is reminiscent of other warnings in Hebrews about the consequences of falling away (cf. 2:1–4; 10:26–31; 12:15–18). The preacher does not need to speculate about the meaning of the words "It is impossible to renew to repentance," which has been the subject of debate for centuries. The author's focus is on the fact that conversion ("being enlightened," 6:4) is a once-for-all event that cannot be repeated. It is probably intended as a warning that people cannot calculate that they can drop out and then return. It is not intended for readers who have fallen away already but for those who are considering it. The image from agriculture (6:7–8) illustrates the message that believers are like the plants that have received a blessing from God, but they must not bear thorns.

The author moves from dire warning to reassurance in 6:9–12, concluding with "in order that you not be sluggish" (6:12). The author motivates the readers by recalling their past acts of love and service (6:10), encouraging them to continue to demonstrate this expression of hope until the end. He will later remind the readers of their many acts of service during the time of persecution (10:32–34).

The entire passage is appropriate for a sermon. Its movement from indictment to warning to confidence in the readers contains a full range of exhortation to the community. Indeed, 6:9–12 is an appropriate positive climax to the sermon, which has spoken negatively of the community. The focus of the sermon on the whole passage is that we may be in a perilous situation because of our failure to develop deep roots (5:11–14), but our past acts of faithfulness motivate us to remain faithful in difficult circumstances. The function of the sermon is to appeal to the readers to grow spiritually, motivating them with a critique of their present situation and a reminder of past acts of faithfulness.

The sermon on this unit may both indict (or confess) our sluggishness in learning (5:11–14) and recall the many good things the church has done (6:9–12) as a motivation for continued spiritual growth in the midst of discouragement. Each subunit within 5:11—6:12 is also a suitable text for preaching. In the indictment in 5:11–14, the sermon reminds us that "you ought to be teachers" is addressed to the whole church rather than to a professional class. The images of ABCs and milk and solid food suggest that personal spiritual growth involves the intellect. Christianity is, at least in part, an intellectual religion. Spiritual-intellectual growth is indispensable for the moral formation (5:14) that equips believers to remain faithful.

Sermon Focus (5:11–14): The path to renewal necessarily involves the engagement of the entire church in intellectual and spiritual growth.

Sermon Function: To urge the community to progress in the knowledge of the Christian faith.

Sermon Sketch: A Forgotten Dimension for the Renewal of the Church

"Drooping hands and weak knees." The phrase from Hebrews (12:12) characterizes not only the first century readers but the fatigue that our own churches face. It suggests the exhaustion of believers who are weary from a journey when the end is not in sight. We have no shortage of proposals for the renewal of the church. But the author of Hebrews mentions a forgotten dimension for the renewal of the church.

1. If the readers of Hebrews have "drooping hands and weak knees," one reason, considering the length of time that they have been Christians, is that they are "dull of hearing." The author has introduced a deep subject—the high priesthood of Christ according to the order of Melchizedek—but concludes that the words are hard to explain, not because of the subject itself but because the readers are like children in the school who have not done their homework. Or to change the metaphor, they have not proceeded from the milk—the elementary teachings—to solid food, the advanced instruction. That is, an exhausted church also suffers from malnutrition. The advanced study, the solid food, is not for the professionals only but for the whole church. Perhaps this is our problem also. The answer for our current lethargy is in developing deep roots in the Christian faith. The author's indictment for his church may be the indictment for the contemporary church.

2. Our answer is "solid food." Ancient teachers described education as the progress from elementary school—the milk—to higher education. Christianity appeals not only to the heart but also to the mind.

3. In a striking athletic metaphor, the author indicates that exercise accompanies good intellectual nutrition. The mature are those "whose faculties have been trained by practice to distinguish good from evil" (Heb 5:14). Just as the athlete trains the body, the whole church trains the mind to distinguish between good and evil. It is constant practice in Bible reading and theological reflection that provides the church with the strength to "hold firmly" to its confession.

The warning in 6:1–8 is an appropriate unit, but its description of the irrevocability of apostasy and the impossibility of restoration presents a special challenge. This is one of three passages that describe the irrevocable consequences of falling away (cf. 10:26–31; 12:15–17). The preacher will probably need to address the readers' theological questions about the impossibility of renewing the apostate, perhaps indicating that this question has been a matter of scholarly debate for centuries. However, the attention should be turned to the rhetorical purpose of the passage. It calls attention first to the blessings received by the listeners; they "tasted the heavenly gift" and "the powers of the coming age" (6:1–2). That is, they have already looked into the future and experienced its blessings, and the foundation for future growth has been laid. Because it was a once-for-all moment, it is unrepeatable; one cannot be renewed to repentance. The passage is not addressed to issues about lapsed Christians desiring to return but to believers who contemplate leaving and then returning. The image from plant life (6:7–8) recalls the frequent use of images from plant life to describe God's people (cf. Jer 1:10; Matt 21:23; 1 Cor 3:6–8). As the image suggests, believers have received blessings from God (6:7), but without proper tending they will experience irrevocable consequences.

Sermon Focus (6:1–8): Like the plant that will wither and die without proper nourishment, believers who have experienced the "powers of the age to come" will wither irrevocably unless they go on to maturity.

Sermon Function: To encourage listeners to go on to maturity, recognizing that the alternative is to fall away irrevocably.

Sermon Sketch: We Stand in the Doorway

Perhaps you have seen the images of Janus, the god of doors. He was usually depicted as having two faces looking at opposite ways, one towards the past and the other towards the future. With his face looking in two directions, he was the god of transitions, a reminder that we all stand in the middle of a narrative. This is especially the case for believers, who look back to the beginning and forward to the end.

1. Beginnings are often the occasions for celebration. Imagine the readers of Hebrews. They could look back to beginnings—the foundation when they learned the first principles of the faith, tasted the heavenly gift, and experienced the powers of the age to come. Many of us can also look back favorably on our beginning of the Christian journey.

2. But we cannot stay at the beginning. In the imagery of Hebrews, what has been planted requires watering and tending. Believers need to go on to maturity, going beyond elementary teachings.

3. The alternative is to fall away irrevocably. As the author of Hebrews explains, the plant that dies unattended cannot be brought back to life. The Jewish philosopher Will Herberg once spoke of our culture as that of a "cut flower." We know what happens when the flower is cut off from its source of life. Thus our challenge is to look back at the

beginning of our journey and recognize that this new beginning can never be repeated.

4. We cannot calculate that we can abandon the faith and return. Scholars may debate the meaning of the author's warning that "it is impossible to renew to repentance" those who fall away, but one thing is clear. We stand in the doorway, and we decide whether we will go on to maturity or make an irrevocable decision to walk away.

The encouraging word of 6:9–12 is also an appropriate text for the sermon. It concludes the extended exhortation that began with "you have become *nōthroi* (NRSV dull) in understanding," and it concludes, "so that you not be *nōthroi* (NRSV sluggish)." While the opening statement points to intellectual dullness, the latter indicates the general sluggishness in their activities. These encouraging words, expressing confidence in the readers (6:9), stand in sharp contrast to the warning in 6:1–8. The passage looks backwards to the community's early days, as in 6:1–2 (cf. 10:32–34), and forward to the end, contrasting the early zeal with the later sluggishness. The author expresses confidence that God will remember (6:9) the community solidarity in love and service in the early days (cf. 10:32–34), and he desires that they maintain the same hope until the end. Only through faithfulness (*pistis*) and patience (*makrothumia*) will the community reach the goal. The motivation for the readers is to recall both their own example from earlier days and the examples of the ancestors who demonstrated faithfulness and endurance. The call for faithfulness and patience is an indication that the community must endure in the midst of its discouragement. The author will later give examples of faithful people who endured (6:13–15; ch. 11).

Sermon Focus (6:9–12): Past experiences of love and service and the example of the ancestors in faith motivate the community to continue in love and good works.

Sermon Function: To express confidence in a discouraged community by recalling our earlier zeal and to encourage listeners not to be overcome by difficult circumstances.

Sermon Sketch: Imitating the Faithful

1. When we suffer from communal exhaustion, memory serves a useful purpose. In our original enthusiasm, we engaged in countless acts of service that, according to the author of Hebrews, God will not

forget. Like the readers of Hebrews, we recall acts of service for one another—the visits to the hospitals, the financial support for the underemployed, the assistance for those who faced tragedy.

2. Such zeal is hard to sustain. We may have compassion fatigue or, as the author of Hebrews describes it, we may become sluggish.

3. We not only look back to our earlier zeal, but also to the faithful people before us. They demonstrated faithfulness and patience (literally, "longsuffering"), the capacity to continue for endless days.

4. The church has faced exhaustion before, and we are still here. I am convinced that another generation of faithful people will come because we were faithful to the end.

6:13—7:28. Exegetical Reflections.

This passage is a continuation from 6:12, "but be imitators of those who through faith and patience inherited the promises." It moves from the example of Abraham (6:13–17) to us (6:18). The entire unit is an assurance to wavering people that we, like Abraham, hold to a promise even if we do not see the results. While the description of the high priest according to the order Melchizedek in chapter 7 appears to stand alone, it is a continuation of the focus on the promise in 6:13–20. Believers have an anchor of hope to hold (6:19) because our forerunner went behind the heavenly curtain, becoming the ultimate high priest—the high priest after the order of Melchizedek (6:20). The image of the anchor indicates that we have something firm to hold on to even when we are wavering. The treatment of Melchizedek in chapter 7 is an elaboration on the anchor that we hold in troubled times. Because this priesthood, unlike the priesthood of Aaron, "abides forever" (7:3, 17, 24, 25), providing believers with the anchor in the midst of uncertainty.

The preacher does not need to speculate about Melchizedek but should recognize the focus of the argument. This high priest is eternal (7:3, 16, 24–25), affirmed by the divine oath "You are a priest forever after the order of Melchizedek" (7:20–21). Just as God swore an oath to Abraham (6:13–15), God has sworn an oath to this ultimate high priest. Indeed, the Christ event is the divine oath. This oath is the guarantee (7:21) of God's fidelity to the promise. Therefore, wavering believers have an anchor in a time of uncertainty in the Christ event, God's guarantee of the future.

Sermon Focus (6:13—7:28): Because God has made an eternal promise, we have something to hold on to (an anchor). Unlike those things in life that we hold on to—things that are temporal—we hold on to the one who is eternal.

Sermon Function: Wavering believers have an assurance of the faithfulness of God to the divine promises. In a world of constant change, the exalted high priest endures forever, giving believers the hope that motivates them to endure.

Sermon Sketch: Hope as the Anchor of the Soul

For most of us, the experiences of the "great generation" are unimaginable, for they—our parents and grandparents—lived through the insecurity of the depression, the dust bowl, and then the war. Savings, property, and jobs were insecure. But for the past generation, jobs, homes, and future plans have been secure until now. A whole society wonders about its future. Things that we thought we could count on can be taken away from us by the pandemic and economic collapse. We wonder what we can hold that is secure.

Our problem is not new. The epistle to the Hebrews, as we have noticed, describes the readers as the new wilderness generation, the people on the way. He also describes them as refugees ("we who have taken refuge") in need of an anchor for their lives. With all the changes and the uncertainty that we face, we, too, look for an anchor.

1. We join faithful people of the past who wait and wait in the insecurity of unfulfilled promises. There was Abraham, who "inherited the promises" only through patience and faithfulness. He found no quick or easy answers, but he waited. We can identify with him.

2. But we have a reason not to waver. If we are adrift with uncertainty, we have the anchor to hold while we wait. The triumph of Christ—his entry behind the curtain—is our anchor of hope.

3. Our anchor of hope is the one thing that cannot be taken away. We may be puzzled about this figure of Melchizedek, but our focus is actually on Jesus, who belongs to the order of Melchizedek. This priesthood is eternal, as the author indicates. While we may be wavering,

we have a guarantee of the future (7:22) in the one who alone abides forever (7:3, 24).

8:1—10:31. Exegetical Reflections.

Because preachers obviously cannot cover all of this passage, they need to see its cumulative effect as it leads toward an exhortation. Chapter 8 continues the message that Jesus is now the heavenly high priest and the guarantor of the new covenant (cf. 7:22) from chapter 7, and chapter 9 describes the entry of Christ into the heavenly sanctuary (9:11–14) and the establishment of the new covenant by the giving of his blood (9:15–22). This sacrifice was once-for-all (9:23—10:18). The dominant focus of this esoteric passage is the finality of the sacrifice of Christ, which has cleansed believers from sin. The citation of Jeremiah 31:31–34, with its promise that "I will remember their sins no more" (Jer 31:34), is the frame of the theological discussion in 8:1—10:18 (cf. Heb 8:12; 10:17–18). The description of the sacrifice of the heavenly high priest in 9:1—10:18 demonstrates that Jeremiah's promise has become a reality in the sacrifice that puts an end to all other sacrifices.

The passage culminates in the exhortation in 10:19. "Having therefore boldness into the entry of the sanctuary by the blood of Christ" summarizes 8:1—10:18. Because of the sacrifice of Christ, the community approaches God "with hearts sprinkled clean from an evil conscience" (10:22). That is, the entry of Christ opened the way for those who follow. The author has earlier described Jesus as the pioneer (2:10) and forerunner (6:20) who opened the way for others to follow. Now our passage indicates that the way into the heavenly world is open for believers. The conclusion is drawn in the exhortation in 10:19–31. Three "let us" clauses draw the conclusions from the theological argument of 8:1—10:18: "Let us draw near with a true heart in the full assurance of faith with our hearts sprinkled from an evil conscience and our bodies washed with pure water" (10:22); "let us hold fast to the confession of hope without wavering" (10:23); "let us stir one another up to love and good works." The latter phrase is followed by "not abandoning the assembly of yourselves together but encouraging one another as you see the day approaching" (10:25). That is, some have already abandoned the assembly. The author is not referring to missing church but to the deliberate abandoning of the assembly, the "deliberate sin" mentioned in 10:26.

The basis for our drawing near, holding on to the confession (v. 23), and "stirring one another up to love and good works" (10:24) is the Christ event described in 8:1—10:18. While other New Testament writers use a variety of images to describe the saving work of Christ for our sins, the author is unique in describing it in Levitical and priestly terms. The work of Christ is a cleansing of the conscience (9:11–14), the "purification for sins" (1:3). It is the reason not to abandon the assembly (10:25). The readers have experienced this cleansing work in baptism—when their bodies "were washed with pure water."

We attend the assembly because the privilege has been given to us by the blood of Christ. To "sin deliberately" (10:26–31)—to abandon the community—is to trample underfoot the blood of Christ that the author has described in chapter 9.

The author has consistently described the Christian life as an exhausting trek under difficult circumstances preceded by the "pioneer" (2:10) and forerunner (6:20) who opened the way into the promised land. This trek is not an individual matter, for only in communal solidarity will the community reach the goal. Indeed, the assembly is the occasion when we "draw near" to the heavenly world in anticipation of the final destination, "stir one another up" and encourage one another.

This lengthy passage offers a variety of ways of approaching the sermon, all of which require that the preacher assumes that the theology leads to the exhortation in 10:19-25. Inasmuch as the central focus in 8:1—10:18 is the removal of sins by the ultimate sacrifice, the sermon could focus on the cleansing that has taken place through the sacrifice of Christ. That "Christ died for our sins" (cf. 1 Cor 15:3) is perhaps the earliest and most basic Christian confession. While New Testament writers employ a variety of metaphors to describe this reality, Hebrews employs the imagery from the sacrificial cult, especially the ritual on the Day of Atonement, in Leviticus.

The passage speaks not only to those who are familiar with the Levitical ritual but to the people of every culture. Cleansing rituals involving sacrifices were common to ancient people everywhere, and they continue today in many cultures. Kwame Bediako in Ghana said that Hebrews was their book with its message that Christ is the end of all sacrifices. While modern listeners may not have the sense of sin, they recognize deep needs for reconciliation. Malcolm Muggeridge said, "The depravity of man is at once the most empirically verifiable reality but at the same time the most intellectually resisted fact."

One may ask "Why go to church?" and begin with Heb 10:25 and then work back to summarize some of 8:1—10:18, describing the saving work of Christ as the extraordinary gift of Christ that opens the way for us to see the future in the midst of our current stress.

Sermon Focus: We remain faithful because we have discovered in the sacrifice of Christ the cleansing that we find nowhere else.

Sermon Function: To remind listeners of the supreme gift, the sacrifice for us, that sustains our commitment.

Sermon: Let Us Draw Near (Heb 10:19–25)

Some years ago, the *Houston Chronicle* had a regular feature in which a critic attended a different worship service each week and offered a critique in its pages. The newspaper had its theater critic, its restaurant critic, and then added its worship service critic. Of course, the critic was not a participant in the worship but an observer. The critic could measure the atmosphere, the professionalism of the musicians, and the effectiveness of the preacher. That is, he measured the worship service by the standards of the theater. By these standards, I assume that few churches measured up.

It is not only the professional worship critic who measures the quality of the service by the standards of the media and the theater. Today people shop for churches to see which worship service meets these standards, and churches compete to measure up to their expectations. A generation ago Neil Postman wrote an important book, entitled *Amusing Ourselves to Death*, in which he maintained that the power of television is such that all communication—education, political discourse, and religion—has been reshaped to meet the demand for entertainment. It is a challenge and a temptation for all of us. Our temptation is to be amateur critics rather than participants. The worship service is not likely to meet the standards of the critic.

Problems with the worship service are as old as the New Testament. I do not know why the original readers of Hebrews were abandoning the assembly, but they are the first ones on record to be encouraged to keep going to church. Those who heard these words had already seen their friends drop out, and they were considering it. The readers had been to many worship services in the little house churches, and nothing seemed to be happening. To be sure, they could not match the pageantry of the local cults, and the atmosphere in the house church could not match what they saw in the great temples.

The author knew that there is something missing in our conversations about worship, and it took him almost ten chapters to explain it. Before he encourages the listeners to be faithful to the assembly, he reorients their thinking, and he has much to say to us. He draws the implications of the majestic vision of the Christ who sits at God's right hand and encourages the listeners to stay in church.

"Having, therefore, confidence to enter the sanctuary by the blood of Jesus . . . by the new and living way opened up through the curtain, and a great priest over the house of God. . ." It is a refrain throughout the book. According to 4:14–16, "Since we have a great high priest who has passed through the heavens, . . . let us draw near." According to 8:1, "We have a high priest who sat down at the right hand of God."

The author recalls the ancient tabernacle where only the high priest could enter, and then only once each year. A curtain separated the most holy place from the holy place and the rest of the world. The author envisions a curtain separating heaven and earth and asks his listeners to catch a vision of the triumphant Christ who opened up the way for the rest of us.

Without his entry to the heavenly sanctuary, the way to God was closed. I understand that this image is remote from us, but I think we can also catch the vision. We come before God because Christ opened the way. If the ancient listeners could see beyond the little group in the house church to know that they were coming before the one who opened the way to heaven, we can see beyond this place to the throne of God.

The most holy place is not behind a curtain in a tabernacle, but wherever we come before God. That is, this is holy ground. Worship is not about us and our desires, but about God. Whatever mood we are in, we come before God. Do you remember that scene when Isaiah saw the Lord on the throne? He heard voices that said, "Holy, holy, holy is the Lord of hosts; the whole earth is filled with his glory." He responded, "I am a man of unclean lips, and I live among people of unclean lips." Or as the author describes the events at Mount Sinai: a blazing fire, and darkness, and gloom, and a tempest, and a terrifying moment when the people asked that no further word be spoken. Then he concludes, "You have come to Mount Zion, the city of the living God, the heavenly Jerusalem." "Our God is a consuming fire."

He has invited us to enter the most holy place. Whether we meet in a pleasant atmosphere, an apartment, or in a storefront, we are in the most holy place. We address our prayers to God because Christ has opened the way. Our songs praise the One who has opened the way. We hear a word from God because the way is open. To worship is to come into the presence of God.

Worship is a gift. You notice how frequently the author says "Since we have." We have a priest who has passed through the heavens, a priest at the right hand of God, and he has opened the way for us. We have a gift of grace. It is by grace that we are here, by grace that we are allowed to worship.

Worship is about God, not about us! How easily we forget that. Imagine the worship wars over catering to the tastes of consumers.

When Isaiah came before God, he said, "Here am I. Send me." I am intrigued by the words of the author, "Let us draw near." In the Old Testament only the high priest was allowed to draw near to God in the sanctuary. Now we all draw near. Worship is not meant for spectators but for participants. Of course, we "draw near" in private prayer. But here we "draw near" together.

Do you know what happens when you come together for worship? "Let us consider how to provoke one another to love and good works." The NIV says, "let us consider how to spur one another to love and good works." Still another translation says, "Let us consider how to rouse one another by love and good works."

When we draw near to God, we draw near to others. Worship does not stop when we leave here. The real test of a good worship service is whether we leave determined to love one another and do good works. It is not necessarily the feelings that we may have, but whether we leave determined to visit the sick, help the poor, volunteer to help others in need.

It takes place here now. But we can do so much more. What if every member asked, "How can I demonstrate love and good works here?" What if we committed ourselves so that no one was overlooked and everyone participated in love and good works?

We look upward and inward but also outward. Paul describes the situation when the visitor comes into the assembly. If the visitor sees only chaos, the visitor will say that you are mad. But if the visitor sees believers praise God and edify one another, the believer will say, "God is in your midst." I am convinced that the outsider who sees us intently praising God and stirring one another up to love and good works will also say, "God is among you."

The amazing growth of early Christianity occurred because believers loved one another as well as others. I am convinced that the only answer for the future of the church is a community that is serious about its worship and stirred up to love one another. We will never measure up to the standards of the theater, but we provide something that is unavailable elsewhere: A people who have been in the presence of God.

The answer is: When we stir one another up to love and good works, we not only care for our brothers and sisters, but we also become lights that lead others to join with us.

Sermon 2: Why Go to Church (Heb 10:19–25)?

I believe that I am safe in saying that the most memorable verse in Hebrews is "Not forsaking the assembly of yourselves together, as is the custom of some." At least it is for me. Before I ever studied anything in Hebrews, I knew the verse. In fact, we were all so familiar with it that most of us could use the shorthand. We would just say, "You know what Hebrews 10:25 says." It seemed that everyone knew.

The verse was also the source of considerable consternation and debate. I remember my first struggle with this verse. I was in the fifth grade, anticipating my first Little League game. I had my new uniform, and I had nailed down my position. A career was in the making. And then the schedules came out. First game: Wednesday night at 8:00. Be there at 7:30. Now that was a crisis. I had a standing appointment at another place Wednesday night at 7:30. Here a promising career could have been stopped before it began because of a schedule conflict. I knew the verse: "Forsake not the assembly." It was also a crisis for my parents, who had to decide where I would be on Wednesday night.

Of course, we had an ongoing conversation about this verse. Which assembly? How many assemblies? What counts as an excused absence? What does "providentially hindered" mean? How many unexcused absences do I get? Does it include when the Cowboys are on? Perhaps you have had the conversation also.

We were missing something with all these questions. Sooner or later we have to ask, why go to church? If you measure the aesthetics of the music by the standards of the philharmonic, in most instances it will not measure up. If we measure the professionalism of the leaders by the standards of the theater, it probably won't measure up here either. If we measure the excitement to a football game, it won't measure up. If we don't come up with some answers, we will see people drifting away. I suppose we have seen people drift away because they just didn't see a reason for going.

That was the problem of the readers of Hebrews. This is the only passage in the New Testament that encourages people to go to church. This is not because attendance is unimportant but because it has only now become a problem. Some were in the habit of neglecting the assembly. If you keep reading about these people, you know the reason. Little by little they had been losing their enthusiasm. Their journey began with so much enthusiasm that they suffered persecution and endured the confiscation of their property with joy. Church attendance was not a problem. Now the interest was fading. Perhaps it was costly in that society to be seen associating with the Christians. They just did not see anything happening in the little house church. You could go down the street to the pagan temples and see something more impressive. Or you could hear the stories of the impressive scene when the high priest went into the holy of holies each year. The little house church could not measure up to what was available elsewhere. The loss of excitement meant they were no longer in the assemblies. I suppose they didn't have a good reason to go.

Does that sound familiar? Haven't we seen that happen? Other commitments seem to become our ultimate commitments, and they squeeze out our time for church. Perhaps we go and we aren't sure why. Or perhaps we find more and more reasons not to go. If you don't know a good reason for going, sooner or later you neglect the assembly more and more.

But why go to church? Have you noticed that the exhortation "not forsaking the assembly" comes near the end of this complicated book? It takes the author that long to get to the most urgent point. I think that I could have gotten to the point more quickly. Everything the author has said has been building toward this exhortation. You wonder if he could have condensed this encouragement to attend church. After all, how many words does it take to say that church attendance is important? But the author knows what we have often missed. There is a reason for attending church. And he takes us through this complicated argument in order to get to this word of encouragement. We could have gotten to the point more quickly, but then we would have missed something. But he wants to tell you why. And before he gets to "not neglecting the assembly," he takes you through the mysterious character Melchizedek and the Levitical sacrificial system and the work of the high priest. Why not just come out and tell us at the beginning that we should be in church?

Why do we attend church? The answer begins with the description of the one who was like us in every respect, died, and was exalted to God's right hand. The author doesn't mention going to church until he has presented this grand story of the exalted one. Probably because that world seemed so remote to readers who could see disappointment and not victories, leaving that world too remote for them. There are times when we, like the original readers, do not see any victories. The only thing that is real is the world that we can see: our careers, our consumer goods, our homes, our status symbols, our political affiliation, our sports teams. Sometimes you notice that they are the only things that are real to us, and they easily become our religions. Someone has commented that the cathedrals today are the sports stadiums. When you travel to older cultures than our own, you see the temples and the old churches that were once the center of religious life. Some of them took centuries to build. If we were to show our cathedrals to the visitors to this country, we could take them to Cowboys stadium. Here you find enthusiasm and religious devotion—at least in some years.

Perhaps the readers of Hebrews wanted something more impressive that they could see. One could visualize and even smell that impressive scene when the priests offered sacrifices for sins. It made people wonder if anything happened at the little house church. But the author of Hebrews offers another perspective. High priests came and went; they died and others took their place. They offered sacrifices, but the sacrifices were repeated year after year. Nothing seemed to last. They are only pale copies of the real high priest who is exalted in the heavens. Visualize a high priest who sits at God's right hand, a high priest who doesn't come and go, but is there forever. Visualize a sacrifice that lasts forever. It has released you from your sins and done something no other sacrifice could ever do. The victorious one is the high priest, but not just an ordinary high priest. He belongs to a different order, the order of Melchizedek, and he lives forever. He serves in a sanctuary that we cannot see. He offered a sacrifice for our sins and put an end to all sacrifices. This high priest is the guarantee of all the promises that God has made to us. Then there is the ministry of the great high priest in the heavenly sanctuary. It's not like any church service that we have ever seen. Then the high priest offers the sacrifice to end all sacrifices—the one that takes away our sins, cleanses our whole being. That is the worship service that takes place in heaven. It is a reminder that Christians believe that what we see is not all that there is.

We do not build our lives on priests that are temporary and sacrifices that do not ultimately cleanse us. Perhaps if the author had been writing today, he would not have written about priests and sanctuaries as the provisional items that we build our lives upon. He might have pointed to our worship of other things—our total commitment to the things that we can see and touch. And he would tell us not to settle for those things that pass away.

We believe that those things that pass away are not all that exists. Someone is high above the substitute religions that we create. What is real is what we cannot see. I am reminded of the poem by the Indian mystic Tagore. He compared our lives to a narrow lane overhung with tall buildings, between which there could be seen above a narrow strip of blue sky torn out of space. The lane, seeing the strip of blue only a few minutes at midday, asks himself, "Is it real?" But then the dust and the rubbish, the jolting carts, the smoke, he concludes, are the real things of life. As for the strip of blue above, he soon ceases to wonder about it, concluding that it is only some kind of mirage. Tagore said that our lives are like that. We accept the things around us—our careers, our homes, our status symbols—as the things that really matter, not recognizing that the strip above is the one thing that lasts forever, the one thing that can orient our lives.

We come to church because we know what is real. Christ has entered into the heavenly sanctuary, and we acknowledge that we build our lives only on the one who abides forever. Only he cleanses our consciences and provides the foundation for our lives. Whether we worship in a grand building, a crowded apartment, or a mud hut, we recognize that we confess that the real world that matters is the one where Christ serves in the heavenly sanctuary.

But it is not only that Christ has entered beyond this world to participate in the heavenly worship service. He has invited us to participate also. "Having therefore the confidence to enter the sanctuary by the blood of Christ, . . . which he opened for us through the curtain . . . and since we have a great priest over the house of God, let us draw near with a true heart in the full assurance of faith with our hearts sprinkled from an evil conscience and our bodies washed with pure water." Yes, it is not just that another reality exists. He has opened the way for us, and our access is only through him. Worship is not ordinary. To worship is to enter the reality that we can build our lives on. We come as recipients of an extraordinary gift—as people who have been given a new life—and we come to accept the invitation of the one who opened the way for us.

"Let us hold firmly to our confession of hope, for he who promises is faithful." It is the grand story that reminds us that we have something to hold on to. We do not hold on to the weak substitutes for our confession of faith, for they will abandon us. We face those moments when our lives are in danger of falling apart, and we reach for an anchor to which we can hold. The one who is eternal gives us an anchor to grasp.

"Let us stir one another up to love and good works." It only happens when you come together, recognize another reality, and know that your love and good works are the only response to the gift that you have received. When we have heard of the gift that we have received, we want to share our love and good works with others. It's nice to hear about the good works done by our members: the work at the Christian Service Center, the prison, the care given to those who face the challenges of illness or bereavement. We do so because we have seen another reality—because we know what is real.

Finally, there is that verse, "Forsaking not the assembly of yourselves together." The author finally got there. And that is a reminder that the good works would not happen without the times when we come together and confess that we see that strip of blue, that heavenly ministry of the one who triumphed over death. And we don't ask about the minimal requirements; nor do we treat it as an onerous obligation, but an opportunity once more to be reminded what is important and what is the anchor of our lives. To worship is to meet with others who share our commitments, and we leave after encouraging one another to love and good works. If Christ has entered that world and invited us to share in it, how could we deny it?

Chapter 3

A CALL FOR ENDURANCE

Hebrews 10:32—13:25

Strangers on the Earth

10:32—12:11. Exegetical Reflections.

THIS EXTENDED SECTION IS too long for a sermon, but it does contain one major idea that might be used for more than one sermon. The key idea is endurance (*hypomonē*), an appropriate word for a community that is in danger of giving up. The author recalls that the community once endured (10:32) and now says, "You need endurance" (10:36). The topic of chapter 11 is faith(fulness), which is the equivalent of endurance in this passage (see 10:36–39). In chapter 12, he says, "Let us run the race with endurance" (12:1) because Jesus endured (12:3). In 12:4–11, he speaks of the community's need for endurance (12:7). The passage can be divided into several sermon texts.

10:32–39. As in 6:9–12, the author motivates the readers by reminding them of their acts of faithfulness in the past. Here he recalls their endurance in the midst of past crises (10:32–34)—abuse, mockery, the care of prisoners, the confiscation of property. The passage is divided into two parts. In the first place, he motivates by recalling the past endurance (10:32–34). That is, like all first-generation movements, this community was willing to endure severe deprivations. They could even endure the loss of possessions because they looked to a better possession in the future. That is, we

45

can endure persecution (10:32–34), but we need to endure when we see no promises being fulfilled.

The author knows of our human capacity to endure suffering as long as there is hope. In the second part, he urges readers who are apparently not being persecuted any more to endure (10:36–39). As members of the second generation, their challenge is to endure, for the readers have waited for promises to be fulfilled, but they do not see the fulfillment of the hopes.

This movement from the community's past to its uncertain future is an appropriate model for preachers, who recognize that their own communities have a history of faithfulness under difficult circumstances, which should motivate them for endurance in the future.

Sermon Focus (10:32–39): Listeners who have endured overt persecution in the past meet the challenge of enduring when the persecution is over by remembering the promise that God has guaranteed.

Sermon Function: To encourage listeners to endure in the midst of marginalization, recalling how they have endured "with joy" in the past, despite overt persecution.

Sermon Sketch: Can We Endure When the Suffering Is Over?

Contemporary believers share with the earliest Christians the marginalization that accompanies the confession that Jesus Christ—not Caesar, not my political party, not my ideology—is Lord. In some places today persecution of believers is an untold story, while in Europe and North America this claim has resulted in marginalization. While believers have endured persecution with joy, the question is: Can we endure when the persecution is over?

1. Believers then and now have endured persecution "with joy" because this commitment was worth dying for. They knew that persecution was not the end of the story. As the author of Hebrews says, they endured the loss of their possessions because they knew of a better possession, a promise for the future. Victor Frankl, who survived a Nazi concentration camp, said it well. "*He* who has a *why to live* for *can* bear *almost any* how."

2. But can we endure when the persecution is over? Can we endure when the boredom sets in? This is the common problem of second-generation movements. This may be the greater challenge.

3. However, like the readers of Hebrews, we wait for a better possession. Or as the author's citation of Habakkuk indicates, we recognize that we live by faithfulness. We do not "shrink back." Just as we endured in earlier times, we endure in all circumstances.

11:1—12:3. Exegetical Observations.

Faithfulness is endurance. The last words of Heb 10 are the transition to the memorable chapter on faith. At the end of chapter 10, the author concludes a section on endurance with the statement that "we are not those who shrink back to destruction, but those who have faith and are saved" (Heb 10:39). Faith(fulness) is thus the opposite of "shrinking back" and the equivalent of endurance.

Chapter 11 illustrates the nature of faith, beginning with a definition (not a full definition, but the definition that is appropriate for this argument). The statement that "faith is the substance of things hoped for, the evidence of things not seen" (11:1 KJV) resumes the thought expressed earlier in 2:8, when the author said, "But we do not see all things in subjection." Here he says that faithfulness is based on what we do not see. Thus the author declares to the community that cannot see the triumph of Christ that the very nature of faith is to see the unseen. It is not a subjective feeling, but the *assurance* of things hoped for, and the *conviction* of things not seen. Life's certainties are not the things that we see, for all these material things are transitory. Believers build their lives on certainty—the unseen things that last forever. The author maintains the focus on "things hoped for" and "things unseen" throughout the catalogue of heroes. Noah looked to things "not yet seen" (11:7), Abraham looked at a distance to the city (11:10, 13), and Moses "saw the invisible one" (11:27).

The heroes of faith illustrate this principle. The author selectively chooses the heroes and their acts of faith. However, among these heroes, the Old Testament attributes faith only to Abraham. In the list of heroes, the author emphasizes to his marginalized audience that building one's life on the unseen inevitably results in marginalization. For example, while Genesis says nothing about Abel's faith, the author speaks of both his faith and his death. In a book that speaks of the offering of sacrifices, Abel is the first to offer a sacrifice. Recalling the story of Abel's death and the words of God to Cain, "Your brother's blood is crying out to me from the ground"

(Gen 4:1), the author declares that Abel still speaks (Heb 11:4). The author returns to the story of Abel later when he declares that the community is now confronted by the blood that speaks greater than the blood of Abel (12:24). Similarly, Enoch and Noah built their lives on the unseen (cf. 11:7). Building one's life on the unseen leads to marginalization, for Noah "condemned the world" (11:7) when he built the ark.

The bulk of the list of heroes focuses on Abraham and his immediate descendants, Isaac, Jacob, and Joseph (11:8–22), and Moses (11:23–31). One may observe that, in keeping with the imagery of the wilderness wanderings, the author makes only passing reference to the people who came after the conquest. The author emphasizes Abraham's marginalization; he "went out," not knowing where he was going (11:8); he was a sojourner living as an alien (11:9). He could take on the marginalization because he built his life on the unseen; he looked to a city "that has foundations whose maker and builder is God" (11:10). Indeed, the author summarizes the story of the patriarchs, indicating that all of them lived as aliens. They were "strangers and pilgrims on the earth" (11:13) while they were looking for a homeland, the city that God has prepared (11:16). In fact, all the heroes of faith suffered deprivation and died without seeing the promises fulfilled (11:13, 39).

The author also demonstrates the nature of Moses's faith in the midst of precarious circumstances. He declined a position in society as Pharaoh's grandson (11:24) but chose instead to suffer the afflictions of Christ. He also built his life on the unseen when he went out as "seeing the invisible one" (11:27). The heroes in 11:32–39 also experienced marginalization and death. Two statements at the end of chapter 11 are worthy of special notice. (1) In 11:39, the author repeats that the heroes of faith never received the promise in their lifetimes, recalling the earlier statement that "these all died in faith, not receiving the promise" (11:13). That is, they built their lives on "things not seen" until the day they died. (2) The last phrase, "without us they would not be made perfect" (11:39), turns to the listeners, indicating that they belong to the list of heroes and that the heroes are depending on them.

In 12:1–3, the author continues his turn to the listeners, describing them as surrounded by a great cloud of witnesses. The image of taking off weights suggests that the readers are in a distance run that requires endurance. Indeed, endurance is mentioned three times in 12:1–3: The author urges the readers, "Let us run the race with endurance," offering as an example Jesus, who "endured the cross" and endured abuse from sinners. This resumes the focus on endurance in 10:32–39. Jesus is the exemplar of faith and endurance under difficult circumstances, but the final result was that he is the pioneer who now sits at the right hand of God and believers will follow him.

We are tempted to build our lives on what we can count and see, but the heroes of faith have always endured when they could not see the results. In fact, Jesus endured in faith before he triumphed.

This section (11:1—12:3) could either be the text for one sermon or a series of sermons around the subject of the faithfulness that results in marginalization. Preachers could reflect on Christian existence in a post-Christian age that is parallel to believers' existence in a pre-Christian age.

Sermon Focus (11:1–7): Faithfulness in difficult circumstances involves taking a stand on things that we cannot see.

Sermon Function: To encourage faithfulness by demonstrating from heroes of the past who have endured by seeing what others cannot see.

Sermon Sketch: "Now Faith Is . . ."

Faith is a distinctively Christian word. The appropriate response to God, according to Jesus and all the New Testament witnesses, is faith. But the word has become so common that we scarcely know what it means. For some, it simply means an opinion, a belief for which we give no evidence. For others, faith is a doctrine, and for others it is simply believing that something is true. Or in the words of Mark Twain, "Faith is believing what you know ain't so."[1]

The author of Hebrews is the only writer in the New Testament who actually defines faith. Surely it is not the only appropriate definition but it is the definition that is appropriate for the circumstances that he addresses. As I first learned it from the KJV, "Faith is the substance of things hoped for, the evidence of things not seen." Having concluded that the Israelites failed to enter the promised land because of their unfaithfulness (*apistia*), he urges his readers not to "shrink back" (10:39) or give up, but to live in faith; or perhaps we should say "faithfulness."

1. Faith is not an opinion, a feeling, or a doctrine. It is a certainty. The KJV accurately renders the word "substance"—sub-stance. That is, a firm

---

1. Cited in Gupta, *Paul and the Language of Faith*, 2.

place to stand, something that is real. We spend our lives looking for that security—personal security, national security, financial security—but it remains elusive.

2. But our place to stand can be found in "things hoped for" and "things unseen," not the places where our culture looks to find certainty and stability. It is not in the visible, tangible things.

3. If you build your lives on "things not seen," you will be strangers in your own culture, the objects of ridicule. As the author of Hebrews recalls the story, Abel offered the right sacrifice, and he was murdered. Noah built the ark and was the object of ridicule. But in so doing he "condemned the world."

4. We endure in difficult times because we are the ones who know what we can build our lives upon. As the author indicates, the people of faith endure marginalization because they know what the culture does not recognize: what is real is not the tangible but "the things not seen."

Sermon Focus: 11:8–16. They died in faith, not seeing the promises.

Sermon Function: To demonstrate that we, like the heroes of faith, see the promises only from a distance while in the present we are "strangers on the earth."

Sermon Sketch: Frustration and Faith

"I see light at the end of the tunnel" is the common mantra of those who want to give an encouraging word in the context of an unending struggle. We heard it in the midst of the pandemic; we have heard it in the midst of endless conflict. Perhaps the declaration in Hebrews that faith is built on "things unseen" sounded like the promise of a light at the end of the tunnel.

1. Faith made the readers strangers in their own land, the objects of ridicule. The author reminds them that all the great heroes of faith were strangers in their own land. It sounded like an endless struggle.

2. But strangers are looking for a homeland. Abraham saw the heavenly city from a distance, building his life on things unseen. Moses suffered abuse because he "saw the invisible one."

3. But they "died in faith, not receiving the promise." We recall those who sacrificed, never seeing the good outcome. And so it is with us. We do not see the fulfillment of the promise. Like the patriarchs, we

discover that we do not see the good outcome for which we work. But we continue because faith is based on "things unseen."

12:1–3. Exegetical Reflections

While the literary style of Heb 11 stands apart from the rest of the homily, the climax of the chapter is actually in 12:1–3. The author makes the transition to this finale in the last line of chapter 11 when he turns from the third person to the first person singular: "without us they would not be made perfect" (or complete). By continuing the first person plural in 12:1–3, he includes his readers in the story of faithfulness. That is, the end of the story depends on them.

According to 12:1–3, the readers are engaged in an athletic contest. Having repeatedly described a strenuous trek in which the readers are involved, the author now uses the athletic imagery that is a common in Jewish literature for the martyrs and frequently used by Paul for the intense struggle in his ministry. The image of the distance run in 12:1–3 suggests the pain of runners who face discouragement and doubt over whether they can finish the course. The author encourages the readers to "fix their eyes" on Jesus, "who for the joy set before him endured the cross" and finished the course and to "consider the one who endured" abuse from sinners. Twice the author emphasizes the *endurance* of Jesus. Only through the endurance of the cross is he now seated at the right hand of God. The author encourages a discouraged people to finish the course, recognizing that their faith began with the one who endured the cross and triumphed.

Sermon Focus (12:1–3): The path to endurance is to consider one who endured shame, abuse, and suffering but finished the course.

Sermon Function: To encourage the community not to give up in the context of disappointment or despair but to look to Jesus, the pioneer who led the way through abuse and the shame of the cross to the ultimate goal, the right hand of God.

Sermon Sketch: Endurance in the Distance Race

Marathon runners speak of the wall of pain that they must work through if they are to finish the course. While some events require speed, the marathon requires endurance through the wall of pain. It is appropriate, then, that the early Christians frequently described their existence as an athletic contest (cf. 1 Cor 9:24–27; Phil 1:30; 1 Thess 2:2). For example, Jewish writers before them described the martyrs as God's athletes. The image suggests sacrifice, opposition, intense self-discipline to the point of exhaustion.

1. It is still an appropriate image for the Christian life. The author of Hebrews comes to the end of his great recitation of the heroes who remained faithful without ever seeing the promise, turning from them to the readers, reminding them that their story is incomplete unless the readers finish the course; "without us they would not be complete." The readers are the athletes who have hit the wall of pain, wondering if they can finish. And so the author says, "Being surrounded by a great cloud of witnesses, let us run the race with endurance." Christian existence is not a sprint but a distance run.

2. But how can we endure the wall of pain? The answer: the ultimate hero of faith is Jesus, our pioneer and perfecter of faithfulness. As a pioneer, he has stood where we stand; he endured the shame of the cross (12:2), and he has endured abuse from sinners. That is, he was the example of endurance in suffering. Our faith did not begin with one who lived in tranquility but one who endured the cross.

3. Looking to Jesus, we see one who not only endured but is seated at the right hand of God. While the great heroes of faith died in faith without seeing the promises, Jesus overcame death and opened the way for those who endure.

4. "So that you not become weary and lose heart" (12:3). It is the vision of the greatest example of faithfulness and endurance that sustains us.

12:4–11. Exegetical Observations.

The author maintains the focus on endurance (v. 7) in the context of suffering, based on the interpretation of Prov 3:11–12. This continues the author's exhortation not to "give out," drawing on a theme that is familiar in Scripture: suffering is a necessary part of *paideia* (vv. 5–7; cf. Deut 8:2–5; Prov 23:13–14). The suffering that is mentioned here is not the misfortune of an individual through illness but the corporate suffering of a community that has been the subject of mob violence and even imprisonment. *Paideia* has a wide range of meanings, including education, discipline, training, and punishment. As a parent may say, "I am going to teach you a lesson." In Greek literature, it was commonly used for education and culture. In Jewish literature, punishment was considered essential to the formation of the child (Prov 23:13–14). This is a word for the group rather than individuals. The community's suffering as a minority group is not a misfortune but serves the purpose of *paideia*.

The image of family is central to this passage. The setting in the original passage in Proverbs is the relationship of a father to his children and the received wisdom that discipline, including punishment, was an essential part of the formation of the child. The author declared that Jesus is God's Son and our brother (2:10–14) and that "we are his house" (3:6); he even indicated that the Son "learned obedience through suffering" (5:8). The author applies the received wisdom about childrearing to the community: "God is speaking to you as sons" (12:5). The author does not suggest that the community's suffering is punishment, but that it is formative, a form of training that will have positive results.

Sermon Focus: At times, communities suffer, and that suffering may have a salutary effect. Believers who suffer join a long caravan of faithful people and are being trained in righteousness.

Sermon Function: To encourage the community to see beyond its present deprivation and to recognize that suffering is not the sign of the absence of God, but of God's act of forming God's children for righteousness.

Sermon Sketch: What is God Teaching Us?

We are accustomed to a culture that treats religion as a consumer product that should make us prosperous and happy. God is the loving Father who wants us to be happy. But then we face reality, as the epistle to the Hebrews reminds us. Believers have found it costly to follow Jesus. They suffer social discrimination and public abuse for their faith. This is still the case in many parts of the world today.

1. For those who accept the view that God wants us to be happy, this suffering is a challenge to faith. We ask how God could allow the innocent to suffer. Many are asking how God could allow a pandemic that ravages the world.

2. But suffering has always been a reality for both believers and unbelievers. Indeed, the author of Hebrews indicates that our suffering is a

discipline and an education. Just as the discipline of the parent forms the child, God's discipline forms disciples. In fact, the word *paideia* can be translated as both *discipline* and *education*. God is teaching us something. C. S. Lewis said that what we want is not a Father in heaven, but a grandfather who indulges us. What we have is a Father who shapes and forms us through suffering.

3. The question is not why God allows us to suffer, but what is God now teaching us in the context of a pandemic?

Going Outside the Camp (12:12—13:25)

12:12–17. Exegetical Reflections.

The image of people on a trek continues in 12:12–17. "Drooping hands and weak knees" characterize those who are exhausted on the trek. This passage has two imperatives for the community on the way. "Make straight paths for your feet, in order that the lame may not be dislocated" suggests that those who are on the trek make special provision for those who are vulnerable; the trek is corporate, and it includes the lame who might be injured by crooked paths. The second imperative, "Pursue holiness . . .," is also addressed to the whole community as the members pursue holiness along the way, without which they will not reach their destination ("to see God"). The participial phrases (in Greek) explain what it means to pursue holiness: "See to it" (*episkopountes*; the noun *episkopos* is the word for bishop; i.e., "we are all bishops" who look out for others):

That no one fail to obtain the grace of God

That no root of bitterness springs up

That no one is immoral like Esau . . ."

That is, all of the people on the trek look out to ensure the cohesion of the group. The Greek repeats *mē tis* (*not any*) three times.

Sermon Focus: Even when we have "drooping hands and weak knees" on our journey, we continue to pursue holiness. But this pursuit is not only a private matter, for we look out not only for ourselves, but also for the lame—the weak and the vulnerable—because every member is a bishop, ensuring that there are no drop-outs.

Sermon Function: To encourage listeners of communal responsibility for the weak and vulnerable in its midst.

Sermon Sketch: *We are all Bishops*

"Pursue holiness," says the author of Hebrews. What images come to mind when we think of pursuing holiness? Spiritual disciplines such as prayer and fasting? Bible reading? These are undoubtedly appropriate spiritual disciplines on the path to holiness. But that is not all. The author of Hebrews envisions a journey in which all have "drooping hands and weak knees." We are exhausted. Undoubtedly, we should look out for our own spiritual well-being.

1. But we are on a trek with others. We are all exhausted, but some are feeble and weak, and the road is treacherous. This is always the nature of Christian community. It includes the chronically ill, the spiritually weak, lonely people.

2. We pursue holiness along the way, but the pursuit of holiness is not a private matter. In fact, we make the treacherous road easier for those who might stumble.

3. As the author of Hebrews indicates, we are all bishops! The author uses the word *episkopountes*, to look out for others. The noun is *episkopos*, bishop. We look out for others, ensuring that no one falls short. Three times the author says to be sure that "not any" fall along the way. The pursuit of holiness is to care for the weakest and most vulnerable.

12:18–29. Exegetical Reflections.

For rhetorical power, this passage is comparable to 1:1–4, serving as the climax of the homily. The passage continues the image of the journey, imagining the audience gathered at a mountain greater than Mount Sinai. In contrast to the frequent exhortations to "draw near" (4:16; 10:23; cf. 7:25; 10:1), here the author says, "You have not drawn near . . ." (12:18). . . . but "you have drawn near" (12:22). To "draw near" recalls the entry of the priests to the altar where they offered sacrifices. It is thus the language of worship in which the whole community participates. The contrast between tangible Mount Sinai and the heavenly Mount Zion, the city of the living God encourages believers to recognize that, although they may not see or feel the effects of worship, they nevertheless experience a more awesome worship. This event is another reason that the community should recognize that it is worth it to be a Christian. Such an awesome event requires a response to God's word (12:25–29). Even if the community that cannot see the awesome event, it has come to something greater than Mount Sinai—and greater than any event that we might imagine.

Sermon Focus: At worship—even when the worship does not appear exciting and we don't feel anything—we are participating in the greatest worship of all. Something happens. Here we pay attention to "the one who is speaking" (12:25).

Sermon Function: To demonstrate that in worship, whether in a majestic cathedral or in a house church, something happens. We encounter the world beyond what we see and touch.

Sermon Sketch: *Did Anything Happen?*

The first church service recorded in the Bible was also the greatest one, and no one would ever forget it. The scene of Israel gathered at Mount Sinai was the first assembly, and no assembly after it would match the impact that it had. The Israelites remembered it forever in their songs and stories. Here was the moment that they received the Ten Commandments. But it was more than that. Our ancestors assembled to hear the word of the Lord, but more happened than they could ever have anticipated. The Lord came down in fire and smoke. There was the blast of the trumpet, the clouds and the thunder. It was such a terrifying event that Moses said, "I tremble with fear." That was quite a church service. Something happened that put the listeners in awe.

There were other moments like this—overpowering moments. Moses encounters God at the burning bush, and he will never be the same. A few centuries later Isaiah enters the temple. He sees the Lord sitting on a throne, high and lofty; and the hem of his robe fills the temple. Seraphs sing, "Holy, holy, holy is the Lord of hosts. The whole earth is full of his glory." Isaiah responds, "Woe is me . . ." It was quite a church service. Something happened that was unforgettable, and it changed his life.

The centuries have passed, and we still assemble before the same Lord. In fact, the most obvious thing we do is to assemble. We have never had an experience quite like that of the Israelites at Mount Sinai or Isaiah in the temple, but we have had moments when something happened, and we were moved by the experience. For many of us, it is the blending of voices together in harmony. I still remember the first time I heard the singing at the first chapel in my freshman year of college. We thought we were hearing angelic voices. We may have had our own "mountaintop experiences." We had moments when we, like those before us, were moved by the experience of worship. It might have been a moment of worship under the stars. Or at an occasion when the sermon spoke to us; or at a time when we could appreciate the beauty of God's creation. We were not at Sinai, but we have been present in worship when something happened.

The reality is, however, that worship is not always like that. We do not always find our pulse quickening, and we do not always have the experience of Israel at Sinai or Isaiah in the temple. We do not always say with Moses, "I tremble with fear." No one can repeat mountaintop experiences week after week. People are assembling around the world today—in stately Gothic churches, in houses, in storefronts, and in mud huts with straw roofs. They do what Christians have done for centuries: they read the Bible, share in the Lord's Supper, sing, and pray. The style of worship may vary from culture to culture, but some things are always the same. Sometimes the setting is not aesthetically pleasing, and often the people cannot retreat into air-conditioned churches where they can seal off the distractions of the outside world. No one confuses their singing with angelic voices nor their worship with Mount Sinai. Nothing seems to happen.

We face a critical problem in our own affluent and entertainment-saturated world. The most pervasive issue among churches throughout North America is the question of what we can do with our assemblies. We come with very high expectations, but the fact that our services are predictable and unchanging creates problems for people who are accustomed to change. We can turn on our television and see dazzling special effects that leave us in awe and hear music that sounds angelic. We experience the drama and the passion of a football game, where electricity runs through the crowd. Here is awe. Then we ask about our assemblies, which can't match the movies or the football stadium for enthusiasm. No wonder that some say that the football stadiums are the cathedrals of North America! Here, in the world of entertainment, something really happens to us.

But does anything happen in worship? We want desperately to recapture in worship that special "mountaintop experience" that we have glimpsed before. Our conversation turns to how we can make something happen. An amazing number of articles and books are being published on what we can do about worship to make it more attractive and to ensure that something happens. We may work with the acoustics of our buildings, experiment with new worship forms, introduce new songs, and change the furniture of our house of worship—all in an effort to "do something" with worship.

It is a good thing to want to renew our worship. It's true that we can learn something about renewing the power of worship. I know that many of us are looking for that experience that leaves us in awe. But I believe there is a missing dimension to the conversation. Today's text addresses this issue and reminds us that our problem is not entirely new. Long ago there was a little house church, probably in a major city. The members were showing signs of apathy, and some were not coming to the assemblies very regularly. The years had passed, and nothing had happened. They had experienced the enthusiasm at the beginning, but now the fire was going out. The assembly in the little house church could not compare with the sights and sounds of the world around them. The members knew about worship in the temple. It was filled with the pageantry of the priests in their robes, the smell of incense, and the sounds of the choral music of the Levites. That was a church service! But all they had now was the little house church. One can doubt the professional qualities of those who led the worship services. Nothing seemed to be happening. Undoubtedly, the members could endure the trials of living in a hostile environment if only something happened in the assembly! They could meet the demands of living a Christian life and the stresses facing the community if only they could see something! But now the years had passed, and some of them were apparently asking it if was worth it to come to the assembly when nothing seemed to be happening.

To make matters worse, the listeners to the letter to the Hebrews now faced hostile neighbors who discriminated against them and threatened their way of life. To face the struggle and weariness of the long pilgrimage with Jesus would be perfect if only they could see and feel something! If only the service could be so overpowering that they could know for sure that the struggle was worth it. I suspect that the author of Hebrews addressed his message to those who barely made it to worship.

The writer speaks a word of encouragement. And then he writes: "You have not come to something that can be touched, a blazing fire, and darkness and gloom, and a tempest, and the sound of a trumpet, and a voice whose words made the hearers beg that no other word be spoken to them." No, we haven't come to repeat the remarkable experience of Sinai. Here in the assembly there is no thunder, no whirlwind. Here, where nothing seems to be happening, we have come to more than that. Here, in the house church, we have come to something that is greater than the first church service. For the ancient community, as for us, worship seems so ordinary with its endless routine.

But, says the author, "You have come to Mount Zion, to the city of the living God, to the heavenly Jerusalem." In the house church—and in our assemblies—we have come to something greater than Sinai. Something is happening! Whether we feel our pulse race or not, whether you feel moved or not, we have come into the presence of God. To meet with God's people is to encounter far more than we can touch or see. Despite what our senses tell us, our worship spans heaven and earth. In worship we encounter the invisible God. As the author of Hebrews says earlier in the sermon, "Faith is the assurance of things hoped for, the conviction of things not seen." Even when we see and feel nothing, we are in the presence of God.

The author of Hebrews does not say that something might happen when the professional performances match our expectations. He does not say that something might happen because of our own creativity. "*You have come* to Mount Zion, the city of the living God." The power of worship does not depend on us, but on the God who has come near in Jesus Christ.

We do not claim that we give no thought to giving our best in worship. Nor do we suggest that forms of worship do not change. But the fact is that we have come to Mount Zion, the heavenly Jerusalem. Our worship is not limited to this place.

To the assembly of twelve in a building meant for 300, he says, "You have come to Mount Zion, the heavenly Jerusalem."

To the assembly in a storefront that cannot escape the distractions of the city, he says, "You have come to Mount Zion."

To a house church in a tenth story apartment in a European city, he says, "You have come to Mount Zion."

To a tiny assembly of eight in a remote rural farming community, he says, "You have come to Mount Zion."

To an assembly of 700 or 1,000 he says, "You have come to Mount Zion, the city of the living God."

Imagine what takes place here. We join in worship with the heavenly world. We are never limited to the house church or our own assembly. In worship we meet with the angels. In worship we come before God, who is the judge of all, and Christ, whose blood speaks to us. Something is really happening.

But worship is more than that. We worship with the universal church. We meet with the "church of the firstborn whose names are written in heaven." We join with the brothers and sisters throughout the world who share in the Lord's Supper on this day. In countless languages, they call on God. Some of you will recall brothers and sisters in Zambia and Kenya. When you share in the Lord's Supper, they are a part of your fellowship. Some of us will recall brothers and sisters in Singapore, Malaysia, and Thailand. Others will recall brothers and sisters in Buenos Aires, Rostov, and Haiti. Something is happening.

But worship is more than that. "You have come to the spirits of the just who have been made perfect." Worship is the occasion when we recall those who have gone before us—that great cloud of witnesses that we know through the Bible and also the great cloud of witnesses who have shaped our faith. We join with Abraham, Isaac, and Jacob. We recall our own teachers in the faith—those who have completed their work. Worship is the occasion for joining them.

And worship is more than that. You have come "to Jesus, the mediator of a new covenant, and to the sprinkled blood that speaks a better word than the blood of Abel." They heard the voice of God at Sinai. When we come to worship, we encounter the crucified Lord, who speaks to us more eloquently than the voice of Abel, "whose blood cried out." We may not hear the voice of God as it shook the earth at Sinai, but in worship we hear the voice of the Christ who addresses us in all circumstances. What an extraordinary experience!

Our temptation with any extraordinary experience is to become so accustomed to it that we no longer recognize or appreciate what we have. I sometimes wonder what it would be like to live in the Alps and to face the Matterhorn day after day; or to visit the Louvre so often as to become so familiar with Michelangelo's David as to no longer appreciate it; or to become so accustomed to the privileges of living in an affluent society with its material privileges that we no longer recognize what we have; or to miss the amazing privilege of meeting with the people of God in worship. The greatest of wonders easily becomes routine for us.

When these experiences become routine, we are tempted to think of this great privilege only in terms of what it does for us. We easily think of worship that way. But the author of Hebrews has a reminder that worship is not about us, for he says, "See that you do not refuse the one who is speaking." The God who provides these privileges is the one who summons us to recognize that he is "a consuming fire." To worship is to come in awe before the creator and judge. Worship is not about us, but about God! When we come before God, something happens.

Hebrews 13

After the grand rhetorical conclusion in 12:18–29, chapter 13 appears to be an appendix. However, the chapter actually summarizes major themes in the book (rhetorical critics call this the *peroratio*). Chapter 13 has three distinct texts for preaching.

13:1–6. Exegetical Observations. These appear to be unconnected imperatives—always a challenge for the preacher. However, the preacher should note that the last lines of chapter 12 speak of acceptable worship (12:28), a theme that is resumed in 13:15–16. In 13:1–6 the author describes acceptable worship in terms of communal behavior. The author has indicated already that believers are outsiders in their own culture. However, outsiders are sustained by robust community life. At the head of the list is *philadelphia* (13:1), a term that was frequently used to describe the identity of the church as a family (cf. Rom 12:10; 1 Thess 4:9–12; 1 Pet 3:8; 2 Pet 1:7). While the term was well known in antiquity for the mutual care of siblings for each other, the Christians appropriated the term to describe a community that was not connected by physical kinship. The author has already recalled the early days when the community demonstrated love by "serving the saints" (6:10) and urged them to "provoke one another with love and good works" (10:24), knowing that a marginalized community is sustained only by the familial care of members for each other. *Philadelphia* is expressed in *philoxenia* (hospitality) and care for prisoners. *Philoxenia* (literally, love for strangers) united the house churches in different cities, permitting believers to find a welcome wherever they traveled. Because marginalization even involves the imprisonment of some (cf. 10:34), believers expose themselves to risk by remembering the prisoners among them. Community solidarity is also expressed in acceptable marriages and the appropriate attitude toward money. The community on the way has a shared moral code as an expression of holiness.

Sermon Focus: Marginalized people are sustained by the bonds of the family of believers, which includes shared moral values and the constant care of members for each other.

Sermon Function: To give concrete examples of the united witness that sustains the community.

Sermon Sketch: *Caring for the Family*

We have seen in Hebrews that people who had been alienated from their families now belong to the family of God. But what does it mean to be family? As a metaphor, the term is often meaningless. If we say that the church is a family, what do we mean? The author of Hebrews concludes the letter speaking of family values in concrete terms.

1. Philadelphia—brotherly love—was used in the ancient world for the love of siblings for each other. But for the early Christians, it was a term used for believers who met in house churches and took over the common roles of the family. We too speak of the church as a loving family.

2. What did does it look like in practice? *Philadelphia*—brotherly love— was expressed in *philoxenia*—love of strangers. We call it hospitality. But it was not the hospitality of inviting your friends for dinner. To be friends to strangers meant inviting strangers from other places into one's home. Hospitality even extended to believers from other places.

3. It also meant caring for prisoners. Some had been imprisoned for their Christian commitment, and believers took the risk of caring for their needs. But that is what it means to be family.

4. It involved shared values toward marriage and money—values that distinguished them from the rest of society. We are a community that honors marital fidelity surrounded by a world where marital vows are too easily disregarded. In a world of greed, we share what we have.

5. Believers who are marginalized in their own society are sustained and united by love, for they have assumed the roles of the best of families—loving care for one another. While we do not limit our loving concern to the larger society, in the church we express the care for those whom we know and see: the aged, the infirm, the disabled. We are family to those who do not have families.

13:7, 17. Exegetical Observations. This passage has the *inclusio* formed by the reference to leaders past and present. "Remember your leaders (13:7)" and "obey and submit to your leaders." After insisting on mutual ministry in the first 12 chapters (cf. 3:12–13; 10:19–25; 12:15–17), the author speaks of leaders. The term (*hēgoumenoi*) is a participle; that is, it is not a title, but a function (cf. Acts 14:12; 15:22). Their task is to "speak the word of God" (13:7) and "watch over souls" (13:17). The two passages that refer to leaders (13:7, 17) are appropriate as a text for preaching. When they are considered in light of chapters 1–12, they indicate the dialectical nature of leadership. While all members encourage each other (3:12; 10:25), some emerge with special tasks. The verbs "remember" (13:7) and "be persuaded and obey" (13:17) indicate the congregational response to leaders who, like shepherds, "watch over" the community.

Sermon Focus: Although we are all responsible for encouraging one another, we also look to those who take the lead in watching out for our souls, reminding us of the faith that we proclaim.

Sermon Function: To remind the listeners that, although we all take responsibility for the spiritual welfare of others, we look to leaders who point the way through word and deed.

Sermon Sketch: Leaders on the Way

We have been disappointed in leaders too many times. Some wanted power and recognition. Others misused a place of trust. Others failed to live up to the ideals they proclaimed. It is enough to make us suspicious of leaders.

1. But we are here because someone first taught us the word of God. But they did not only teach through words; they were faithful in deeds until the end of their lives. Indeed, the great heroes of the faith are not just the ones we read about in Heb 11, but the people we have actually known. While we may be disappointed in leaders at times, we recall those who embodied the faith that they taught, and our task is to imitate them.

2. But our leaders are not only distant memories. While we all take responsibility for the welfare of the community, we honor those who are called for the special task of seeking our welfare. In the words of the author of Hebrews, "they watch over our souls," and they will give an account for how they have executed their task.

3. We remember the leaders in the past (13:7), and we "obey and sub-mit" to the leaders in the present so that they may conduct themselves with joy. Of course, we do not "obey and submit" to all leaders in all circumstances, but we recognize our need for leaders who guide us.

13:8-16. Exegetical Observations. The reference to the leaders in 13:7, 17 is the bookend for the author's final exhortation to the church. The material in 13:8–16 reiterates the substance of our faith, summarizing the basic argument of the entire homily. It is so condensed that almost every line has been the subject of debate; that is, what are the "diverse and strange teachings" (13:9)? The author does not identify them; the hom-ily has not mentioned them previously. What is the altar that "we have" (13:10)? Who are those who now "serve in the tent" (13:10)? The preacher cannot resolve these issues, but should discover the rhetorical focus of the passage and its inner logic. This section follows the normal stylistic pattern of the author, in which what "we have" (13:10, 14) is the basis for the exhortation "let us" (13:13, 15–16).

The epigrammatic "Jesus Christ is the same yesterday, today, and for-ever" (13:8) recalls the homily's consistent claim that the exalted Christ is "the same" (1:12), and that he abides forever (1:11; 7:3, 24–25). He stands in contrast to the diverse teachings to which the listeners may be exposed (13:9). The author gives the true teaching in 13:10–11. That is, "we have an altar" that no one else has (13:10). It is the suffering of Jesus "outside the gate" (13:12). While the statement is literally a recollection that Jesus died outside the city gates of Jerusalem (John 19:17, 20), it has a deeper meaning, as the exhortation that follows in 13:13 indicates. This is a reminder of Heb 9:11–14, which describes the sacrifice of Christ in the heavenly sanctuary. Indeed, "we have an altar" reminds us of the previous statements that "we have a great high priest" (4:14; 8:1; 10:19–23). The focus of Jesus's death "outside the gate" is the encouragement for believers to "go to him outside the camp, bearing his shame" (13:13). As the book has frequently reminded us, the believers are marginalized in their own society. The author encour-ages readers to "go outside" of their comfortable place and live as strangers in the world, as the patriarchs had done earlier (11:13–16). In following Jesus "outside the camp" and into the place of shame, they follow Jesus the pioneer whose death outside the camp resulted in his exaltation to God's right hand. Those who follow Jesus "outside the camp" of their own culture recognize that they, like the patriarchs before them, have an abiding city.

Sermon Focus (Heb 13:9–13): The encouragement to follow Jesus "outside the camp" is a reminder that marginalization is not an unfortunate circumstance, but the very nature of discipleship. Just as Jesus suffered as the marginalized one, believers can also expect to be marginalized.

Sermon Function: To encourage believers to accept the challenge of living in a post-Christian world of marginalization, knowing that the Christian faith began with the marginalized one.

Sermon Sketch: *Let Us Go outside the Camp*

"Why are you a Christian?" an old friend asked me. "You are educated, but you are nevertheless a Christian." For him, being a Christian was like believing in a flat earth. I was thirty years old, in the final stages of writing a doctoral dissertation, and no one had ever asked me that question before. After all, everyone was a Christian. We lived in a Christian nation, and the majority of people identified themselves as Christians. But, as I realized that day, the world is changing, and we now live in a post-Christian world.

I suppose it was easy being a Christian in a Christian society. But how is a Christian to live in a post-Christian society? We may not be overtly persecuted, but we may be the objects of disdain and marginalization.

1. That situation is not new. The believer in a post-Christian society can learn from believers in a pre-Christian society. We learn from the message of the author of Hebrews to readers who had suffered the confiscation of their property and even imprisonment. It is the consistent message of the New Testament. To become a Christian is costly because it alienates believers from family and friends. The heroes of faith in Heb 11 were all outsiders—strangers and pilgrims—in their own land. In the twentieth century, Ernst Käsemann wrote his influential book on Hebrews, *The Wandering People of God*, from prison because he identified with the strangers and aliens in Hebrews.

2. But Christianity began with the ultimate outsider. Jesus died "outside the camp," the place where the remains of sacrifices were buried. It became the place where criminals were executed. As George McLeod eloquently said, "I simply argue that the cross be raised again at the center of the marketplace as well as on the steeple of the church. I am recovering the claim that Jesus was not crucified in a cathedral between two candles, but on a cross between two thieves; on the town garbage heap; at a crossroads so cosmopolitan that they had to write his title in

Hebrew and in Latin and in Greek . . . at the kind of place where cynics talk smut and thieves curse, and soldiers gamble. Because that is where he died. And that is what he died about. . . . That is where churchmen ought to be and what churchmen ought to be about."

3. Where do believers belong? "Let us then go to him outside the camp." Like the patriarchs, the believers "go out," knowing that marginalized people have a city (13:14; cf. 11:10). To be "outside the camp" is not an unfortunate circumstance, but the path of our Savior.

Hebrews 13:14–16. Exegetical Observations.

Apparently, to "go out" of the place of comfort and acceptance by the society is also to turn inward to the community in worship and good deeds (13:15–16), for the author's last exhortation is twofold: a) "Let us continually offer up a sacrifice of praise to God" b) "do not neglect to do good and to share what you have, for such sacrifices are pleasing to God." This final exhortation is a fitting conclusion to the homily. Having declared that Jesus offered the ultimate sacrifice, the author mentions two forms of sacrifice by believers: worship and good deeds.

Sermon Focus (13:15–16): As a people who, like the patriarchs, look to the "abiding city" (13:14), believers offer acceptable worship in praise and good deeds.

Sermon Function (13:15–16): To urge the community to recognize that hope for the future is the motivation for a sacrificial response to God in the present in the form of praise and good deeds.

Sermon Sketch: True Worship

The "worship wars" have come to almost all churches, often creating divisions between the generations. All participants come with their own ideas of what worship should be, looking to diverse models of worship. Some favor the sense of awe in a liturgical service, while others favor a more theatrical presentation. After a lengthy section on worship, the author concludes the homily describing acceptable worship (cf. 12:28; 13:16). What is an appropriate worship service? One wonders about the criteria for determining the quality of the service. People naturally judge the service with the criteria from other public events.

1. The epistle to the Hebrews spends the major part of the homily discussing the offering of sacrifices by the priest. Indeed, his contemporaries expressed awe at the visual sight of the priest in his robes entering into the temple each year. It was surely an awesome sight.

2. But the author concludes with an observation of acceptable worship that is not what we would have expected or the way we would have defined proper worship. First there is the sacrifice of praise; perhaps he has in mind something like the opening words of the homily, which are likely an early Christian hymn. Then there are the good deeds and the fellowship—*koinōnia*—of the community, the sharing of possessions and the common life of the group.

3. The author of Hebrews reminds us that acceptable worship occurs both inside and outside our assemblies. We respond to the sacrifice of Christ, not with a worship that fits our tastes, but with our own sacrifice of praise and good deeds.

1 PETER

A BRIEF INTRODUCTION
TO 1 PETER

As I INDICATED IN my reflections on Hebrews, some books of the New Testament lie in obscurity until their message is rediscovered as a word spoken to our own circumstances. In the past generation, scholars have recognized that Hebrews is not merely a book containing esoteric arguments but a word spoken to "the wandering people of God"—those who are homeless in their own culture and looking for a homeland. Indeed, the great heroes of the faith were, according to the author, "strangers on the earth" (Heb 11:13) and models for readers whom the author urges to go "outside the camp" of their own culture. Similarly, 1 Peter has emerged from obscurity in the last generation because this word, addressed to "exiles of the dispersion" (1:1) in a pre-Christian world, also speaks to Christian exiles of a post-Christian culture. Thus 1 Peter and Hebrews are combined in this volume because they both speak to marginalized believers who have discovered the cost of their Christian commitment.

The letter is addressed to "the exiles of the dispersion in Pontus, Galatia, Cappadocia, Asia, and Bithynia"—a land mass that includes regions that comprise a major part of present-day Turkey. The date and the circumstances of the writing are matters of debate. The author, who identifies himself as Peter, writes from "Babylon" (5:12), which is probably a coded reference to Rome (cf. Rev 14:2; 17:5; 18:2). The consistent themes of exile (1:1, 17; 2:11; cf. 4:4) and suffering (2:19–20; 3:14, 17; 4:1, 15, 19; 5:10) throughout the letter are central issues for determining both the authorship and date of the book, indicating that the occasion of the letter is a time of persecution. However, scholars debate the nature of the persecution. If Peter is the author, the occasion of 1 Peter is the official persecution under Nero (ca. AD 64). However, since the persecution under Nero was largely limited to Rome, others have suggested that persecutions under either Domitian (AD 81–96) or Trajan (ca. 110) were the background of 1 Peter.[1] Most of the references in 1 Peter, however, do not suggest that the suffering of believers was initiated by the authorities but consists of the continuing discrimination and slander (2:12, 16) against Christians because of their withdrawal from the civic and the cultural life in their respective cities (cf. 4:4) as well as the divisions they created within families (1 Pet 2:18–25; 3:1–7). This kind of harassment was common in the first century, as Paul's epistles demonstrate (cf. Phil 1:28–29; 2 Cor 1:6–7). The worship of a Savior convicted of offenses against the state ensured the hostility of the populace in each region.

However, the advice to those who "suffer as Christians" may suggest a more official form of persecution. Indeed, to "suffer as a Christian" (4:16) apparently involves suffering simply because of the name *Christian*. This suffering fits well with the later persecution under Domitian, who was emperor from AD 81 to 96. Some have even associated the persecution with the period of Trajan (AD 98–117), whose correspondence with Pliny is a mirror into the conflict between the Roman government and the Christians in the early second century. Pliny, the governor of Bithynia, one of the regions addressed in 1 Peter, writes to Trajan, inquiring about the punishment given to those who bear the name "Christian."

Pliny writes:

> It is my custom to refer all my difficulties to you, Sir, for no one is better able to resolve my doubts and to inform my ignorance. I have never been present at an examination of Christians. Consequently, I do not know the nature or the extent of the punishments usually meted out to them, nor the grounds for starting an investigation and how far it should be pressed (Pliny, *Ep.* 10.96).

Pliny's letter, indicating that believers were persecuted for no other charge than being Christians, corresponds to the reference to anyone who "suffers as a Christian" in 1 Peter.

Although both the date and the identity of the author are debatable, in this book I shall refer to the author as Peter, the implied author. Our

---

1. See Schnelle, *First Hundred Years of Christianity*, 441–42.

interpretation does not depend on the actual authorship, but on the witness of 1 Peter to the struggles that believers have repeatedly faced throughout the history of Christianity. The letter consistently addresses the tenuous place of believers in their own society. Twice the author addresses them as aliens (*parepidēmoi*, 1:1; 2:11), using the term that commonly referred to resident aliens. He also addresses them as exiles (*paroikoi*), a term that literally means homeless (1:17; 2:11). These terms comprised the dominant metaphor to describe the Christian's relation to society.[2] This image resonates throughout the history of Christianity.[3] Until the Constantinian era, which began in AD 313, the image characterized the place of Christians in the world. One needs only to recall the impact of Dietrich Bonhoeffer's *The Cost of Discipleship* and the accounts of life in a totalitarian society. Martin Niemöller was imprisoned in Berlin because he rejected the interference of the Nazis in the affairs of the Protestant Church. Under Nazi pressure, the German church had passed a resolution barring anyone with Jewish ancestry from being ordained to the ministry. Niemöller resisted the Nazi pressure and openly spoke out against the resolution. He wrote to his wife from prison, "We do not want to forget that even the German fatherland means a foreign exile to us, as for the man who had nothing as he lay in the manger because he laid down his head out of love for the people."[4]

The metaphor of "aliens" has a powerful influence because it sums up central themes from the Old Testament and expresses fundamental realities about the life of faith. Abraham was called from his own country, his relatives, and his father's house (Gen 12:1). His grandchildren and their grandchildren became "aliens in the land of Egypt" (Lev 19:34). Even when Israel was in its own land, they were instructed "not to do as they do in the land of Egypt," and "not [to] do as they do in the land of Canaan" (Lev 18:3). The nation then lost its land and lived as aliens in captivity.[5] The ultimate alien was Jesus, who "came into his own and his own received him not" (John 1:10).

Exiles were commonly identifiable by the language, customs, and skin color of their homeland. Because they were aliens and exiles, they did not have the rights of citizenship. Consequently, they were vulnerable to abuse and persecution. The exiles of 1 Peter, however, were not

---

2. Feldmeier, *Die Christen als Fremde.*

3. See Volf, "Soft Difference," 16–17.

4. Niemöller, *Exile in the Fatherland,* 124.

5. Volf, "Soft Difference," 17.

identifiable by their language or national customs but by their allegiance to Christ and their way of life. Their allegiance to Christ raised suspicions about their allegiance to the caesar (cf. 2:13–17) and adherence to the established order of society, including the submission of slaves to their masters (2:18–25) and wives to their husbands (3:1–7). The author indicates that "they are surprised that you no longer join them in the same excesses of dissipation, and so they blaspheme" (4:4). Indeed, the readers are frequently charged with undermining civic life; the local populace criticizes them as "evildoers" (cf. 2:12).

The frequent references to the community's suffering indicate the pain of the exile existence. Believers are now suffering various trials that test the genuineness of their faith (1:6). They are suffering for doing good (2:20; 3:17); thus they are sharing the sufferings of Christ (4:13). They do not suffer because of their wrongdoing, but they "suffer as Christians" (4:16) in the conviction that God will restore them after their period of suffering (5:10).

Although the themes of exile and suffering appear throughout the letter, Peter indicates the actual purpose of the letter at the conclusion: "I have written this short letter to encourage you and to testify that this is the true grace of God. Stand in it" (5:12). Peter speaks of exile and suffering in the context of hope. The believers have been "born again to a living hope" (1:3; cf. 1:21; 1:9), which is founded on the triumph of Christ at the resurrection (1:3, 3:21–22). Thus their suffering is the path of the One who suffered and was raised from the dead. The readers now live in a time of testing, but the test is the prelude to ultimate salvation. Because of this living hope, believers may now "stand" in the grace of God (5:12).

First Peter speaks with power to all who experience the exile existence, for marginalization can lead to resignation, hopelessness, or to the temptation to assimilate once more into the dominant culture. For believers who are marginalized, it is a reminder that the Christian faith began with the suffering Savior and that we live in hope for the future. For believers who have been coopted by the dominant culture, it is a reminder that to walk "in his steps" is to resist these temptations.

First Peter speaks especially to believers who live in the transition from a Constantinian culture to a post-Constantinian environment. The Constantinian culture began with the Edict of Milan in 313, which declared Christianity the official religion of the empire, and is now coming to the end in a post-Christian culture. This transition is deeply disturbing to believers who had once lived comfortably with the public support of the Christian faith and a Christian consensus in which it appeared that everyone was a Christian. With the decline of church membership and the loss of a Christian culture, believers in a post-Christian culture can identify with those in a pre-Christian culture. Thus 1 Peter speaks to Christians who are exiles in their own land, encouraging them to stand firmly and reminding them that the exile existence is no unfortunate tragedy but a calling to "be holy as God is holy" (1:16; cf. Lev 19:2). The people of God are called to separate themselves from the dominant culture in order to be a blessing to it.

Like Hebrews, 1 Peter is a word of encouragement (cf. 1 Pet 5:12; cf. Heb 13:22). Unlike Hebrews, however, 1 Peter has no extended argument. Thus the structure is elusive inasmuch as it consists of a series of exhortations. After the opening blessing (1:3–12), these exhortations consist of an imperative followed by a theological reason. Each of these units is part of the mosaic of this letter, and each of these texts is suitable for preaching. All the imperatives are spoken to people who live as exiles and offer encouragement to conduct themselves in a way appropriate to their situation.

A CALL TO BE HOLY

1 Peter 1:1—2:10

1 Peter 1:3–12. Exegetical Observations. "Blessed be the God and Father of the Lord Jesus Christ!" These are the frequent words of the Psalmist, who praises God for saving deeds. In the New Testament, Zechariah responded with these words when he was promised the son who would call Israel to repentance (Luke 1:68). Paul normally begins his letters with a thanksgiving but twice began with "Blessed be the God and Father of our Lord Jesus Christ, who" (2 Cor 1:3; Eph 1:3). First Peter also begins with these words of praise.

Opening words are important for any message. Ancient orators knew that the exordium, the opening words of a speech, should introduce the topic and make the audience favorably disposed. The opening words of 1 Peter fulfill both requirements. The author acknowledges that the readers now "suffer various trials" (1:6), having already addressed them as "exiles of the dispersion" (1:1). The themes of exile and suffering continue throughout the letter. However, the passage rings with praise and celebration. The community's suffering is not the occasion for mourning, but for rejoicing. Indeed, the author twice declares that the community now rejoices (1:6, 8), and the entire pericope demonstrates that, while the culture may consider celebration and rejoicing as the appropriate response to good news or major transitions in life, believers celebrate in the context of suffering. They celebrate because they have been born to a living hope through the resurrection of the dead (1:3–5, 9). Indeed, they also celebrate because they stand at the culmination of all the hopes of the faithful people of the past

(1:10–12). Consequently, they see their suffering in a new light; they are, like precious metals, being tested by fire. Thus their celebration is not that of their pagan neighbors, who live in "licentiousness, passions, drunkenness, revels, carousing, and lawless idolatry" (4:4). The initial response to the community's suffering is praise.

Merging the Horizons: The preacher's task is not merely to explain the text but to evoke its celebratory mood, interpreting both the text and the congregation. Congregations that experience marginalization can identify with the experience of the first readers and be encouraged to see beyond their vulnerable existence to celebrate their place in God's plan. Affluent congregations will be called upon to recognize that only through placing themselves over against culture will they find the true cause for celebration.

Sermon Focus: We rejoice in our suffering (or any form of testing) because we have received what prophets and angels longed to see and we know that hope lies beyond the present distress.

Sermon Function: To lead the congregation in praise under difficult circumstances.

Sermon Sketch: Praise Music

"How do we sing the Lord's song in a foreign land?" asked the Psalmist (137:4). People in exile do not feel like singing. We understand the sentiment. We enjoy singing when circumstances for us are good. Praise to God seems natural when we see God's gifts all around us.

1. But as Peter demonstrates, believers may sing praise in dire circumstances. Having addressed "exiles of the dispersion" (1:1), he opens a letter to suffering believers with a song of praise: "Blessed be the God and Father of our Lord Jesus Christ." During the Easter week of 1945, Dietrich Bonhoeffer led his fellow prisoners in worship at the prison camp in Schönberg, where he had been a constant source of encouragement. He read from 1 Pet 1:3, "Blessed be the God of our Lord Jesus Christ! By his great mercy we have been born anew to a living hope through the resurrection of Jesus from the dead." After Bonhoeffer had spoken for a few minutes on the meaning of those ancient words for their situation, the prison doors opened, and two sinister men entered the cell and said, "Prisoner Bonhoeffer, get ready to go with us." Everyone knew what those words meant. Bonhoeffer went to his execution

on the cold day of April 9, 1945.[1] He had found a special meaning to the opening words of 1 Peter. He taught us that we do not respond to suffering with despair, but with praise.

2. It is praise that we have been born again to a living hope. As Peter indicates twice in this song of praise, we rejoice because we—not those who are at ease in their culture—are the privileged ones. Our rejoicing is not that of our culture—the joy over trivial things. It is the joy that we now have what prophets anticipated and what angels longed to see. We rejoice even while we are being tested because we see beyond the momentary suffering.

3. We see beyond the momentary affliction. As we follow the one who suffered, we also follow the one who triumphed over death. We have reason to sing. Singing is a major part of what we do as a community. Like the Psalmists, we sing to celebrate good news and we sing under the most difficult circumstances. Even during the pandemic, we sing, "Blessed be the God and father of our Lord Jesus Christ."

1 Peter 1:13–25. Exegetical Observations. In the opening words of the epistle, Peter praises God that we have "been born again to a living hope by the resurrection of Jesus Christ from the dead, an inheritance that is imperishable, undefiled, and unfading" (1:3–4). This hope sustains a distressed community. The importance of hope is indicated by the first imperative of the book: "Set your hope on the grace that Jesus Christ will bring you when he is revealed" at his revelation (1:13). Near the end of the passage, Peter says, "So that your faith and your hope may be in God" (1:21). The repeated appeal to the community's hope indicates the extent to which hope is the basis for the exhortations. As the first in a series of imperatives in a letter to suffering Christians, Peter points to the hope that is the motivation for all the instructions that follow.

The readers are motivated not only by hope for what God will do in the future but also on what God has done in the past, for "therefore" (1:13) links the imperative with the reminder that even angels longed to see what they now experience (1:12). After the first imperative, Peter recalls that believers were "ransomed" with precious blood (1:18–20). Thus the readers live in the interim between what God has done and what God will do in the future.

This hope in the midst of the exile existence gives urgency to the community's moral conduct, for it is their moral conduct that makes

---

1. Willimon, *Gospel for the Person Who Has Everything,* 59.

them aliens. Few translations indicate the sense of urgency that follows "therefore" in 1:13. While the NRSV has "prepare your minds," the literal translation is "girding up the loins of your minds." The image of girding the loins evokes the image of individuals who wear flowing robes, which they must bind before they do strenuous activity. The image recalls the exodus story when the Israelites were instructed to gird their loins to be ready for their sudden departure from Egypt and Jesus's instruction to the disciples to "be dressed for action" (literally, "gird your loins") and have your lamps lit; be like those who are waiting for their master to return from the wedding banquet" (Luke 12:35). Thus the image indicates the urgency of appropriate conduct for those who live with suffering in the interim between God's saving acts in the past and the realization of the Christian hope. The unusual image of girding up "the loins of the mind" indicates the concentration that is necessary for believers. The image is reminiscent of the frequent summons in the New Testament to "stay awake" (cf. 1 Cor 16:13; 1 Thess 5:6, 10). The exile existence is not a casual matter; it demands constant vigilance.

As the passage indicates, the readers hope in a "time of exile" (1:17) and have abandoned the "traditions of the fathers" (1:18). In a culture in which religion and family were so connected, the readers are now separated from their ancestral ties. However, as Peter indicates, this separation is not a misfortune but the very calling of the community. They have abandoned their former behavior and the society around them. Now Peter reminds them that their separation is the very nature of discipleship. In calling them to be holy, he cites Lev 19:2, connecting the readers with Israel and Israel's mission to be separate from the nations around them.

When Peter says "You were ransomed from the futile ways of your fathers" (1:18), he gives a further indication that the community's suffering is not a misfortune. Despite the pain that they experience in being alienated from their families, the community knows that it has been "ransomed" with something more precious than gold. The community lives in the interim between God's saving act in the past and the hope for the future.

Indeed, like other New Testament writers, Peter regards hope as foundation for the moral life. Following the Levitical code, Peter indicates two dimensions of holy living. In the first place, it involves abandoning their former enslavement to the passions—the sexual mores of the wider culture (1:14). This instruction conforms to the holiness code of Lev 18–19 and is commonplace in early Christian moral instruction.

In the second place, their challenge is to practice "brotherly love" (1:22). Those who have been abandoned by their physical families now have a new family. This term was used in antiquity for the love between actual siblings, but Peter applies it to the community. That is, exiles separated from their families now have a new family.

Merging the Horizons: In our post-Constantinian world, we may be surprised that our culture no longer supports our way of life, leaving us as exiles in our own land. Our insistence on marital fidelity, compassion for the poor, and the sanctity of life may separate us from a society that has little moral anchor. Furthermore, while ancient readers were alienated from their close relationships by their rejection of their families' basic worldview, modern readers are also frequently uprooted from their families and friends in another way. The mobility of modern society has left them without meaningful relationships. The exile community rediscovers a new family that practices holiness, not as a misfortune but as God's calling. Holiness may separate us from our culture, but it is lived within a new family, sustained by hope.

Sermon Focus: Hope sustains exiles and motivates them for holy living, which consists of turning away from the society's mores and turning toward the new family.

Sermon Function: To encourage listeners to continue as a counterculture—a holy people—as they live in hope and in solidarity with the new family.

Sermon Sketch: Is That All There Is?

"Is that all there is?" is a refrain that was popularized in a song in the 1960s, but the theme originated much earlier in the work of German writer Thomas Mann. According to one verse of the song,

> Is that all there is?
>
> Is that all there is?
>
> If that's all there is, my friends, then let's keep dancing
>
> Let's break out the booze and have a ball
>
> If that's all there is.

The song continues to be replayed in our culture. It is the voice of disillusionment that dominates our culture. Hope is difficult to find amid the threats of climate change, pandemic, and economic collapse. Where can we find hope in our culture? According to 1 Peter, those who hope are the ones who see nothing around them but discrimination and marginalization.

1. Those who live in hope know that this is not "all there is" and that this knowledge gives urgency for us to make the best of our limited time in the interim between what God has done in the past and what God will do in the future. As Peter says, angels longed to see what we now see (1:12). We have been ransomed (1:18) with a precious price. Yet God has not finished with us, for we recognize that God raised Jesus from the dead (1:21) and promises to vindicate us in the future. "Prepare yourselves"—literally "gird up the loins of your mind" —like the ancient people who bound their robes for work. I recall someone who said that this is no "slouch religion." It is demanding.

2. It summons us to reject the lifestyle and the sexual mores of our culture—in Peter's words, not to be conformed to the passions that characterized their previous lives (1:14). Like Israel, we are called to "be holy as God is holy"; that is, to separate ourselves from the vices of our culture and be devoted to the God who is holy.

3. But exiles who have been rejected by their own families turn to their new family. "Brotherly love"—*philadelphia*—was used in antiquity only for the mutual care of siblings. But the exile community lives in a new family.

First Peter 2:1–10. Exegetical Observations. The *Epistle of Diognetus*, written in the early second century, speaks to a pagan audience, describing Christians. The writer says, "Christians are not distinguished from the rest of humanity by country, language or custom" (5:1). Then the author adds, "They live in their own countries, but only as nonresidents" (5:5). The readers of 1 Peter could identify with these words, for they were exiles, not because of their language or color of skin but because of their Christian commitment. When Peter says, "Rid yourselves, therefore, of all malice, guile, envy, and slander," he is actually using a verb that was employed for taking off one's clothes (*apotithemi*), an image that was commonplace in instructions to new converts (cf. Rom 13:12; Eph 4:22; Col 3:8). That is, old habits that had been commonplace in the culture and had been shared by the readers are now to be stripped off like an old set of clothes.

According to 1 Peter, believers were exiles because of their moral conduct (cf. 1 Pet 4:4). Their situation is similar to that described in the *Epistle of Diognetus*.

They marry like everyone else, and have children, but they do not expose their offspring. They share their food but not their wives. They are in the flesh, but they do not live according to the flesh. They live on earth, but their citizenship is in heaven. They obey the established laws; indeed in their private lives they transcend the laws" (5:6–9).

The readers of 1 Peter are "newborn infants," recent converts who will grow into salvation as they are nourished on the milk of Christian instruction (2:2). They can rid themselves of old habits only if they have a place to turn. Thus Peter says, "Come to him, the living stone, rejected by men but chosen by God, and be yourselves built into a spiritual house to offer sacrifices to God" (2:4). Changing the metaphors, Peter encourages the readers, indicating that their task is to follow Jesus, the first exile. He was rejected by the populace but chosen by God. Indeed, Peter brings together two passages from Scripture to illustrate his point. On the one hand, there is "the cornerstone chosen and precious" (1 Pet 2:6; cf. Isa 28:16); on the other hand, there is the "stone that the builders rejected" (2:7; cf. Ps 118:22), a stone of stumbling (2:8; cf. Isa 8:14). That is, while others have rejected the living stone, Christians believe in the one who has become the cornerstone, the one chosen by God. Indeed, the one rejected by humankind is God's chosen.

Exile existence is not a solitary matter. Believers are being "built together" into a spiritual house (2:5), of which Christ is the cornerstone. They share his exile existence, building a house that can be done only as a community. Indeed, as they follow the first exile, God's chosen one; they are "an elect race, a royal priesthood" (2:9).

Merging the Horizons: As the repetition of the term *elect* (or *chosen* in some translations) indicates (2:4, 6, 9), the focus of the passage is the special place of the community in God's plan. This passage is an assurance to those who suffer from marginalization and persecution, having lost their place in society. Like the Savior before them, they are rejected by the people but chosen by God. Despite all appearances, they are the privileged ones. They do not retreat from society, however, but they proclaim the mighty acts of the God who called them. As Peter indicates in 2:9, exiles engage in mission to the world, as Donald Senior commented:

> One of the major contributions of 1 Peter is the robust sense of Christian mission he conveys. Even though these fragile communities are embedded in a hostile environment and suffering abuse,

he does not prescribe reaction or caution. The Christians are not to flee the world but to participate in it (2:13). They are not to condemn or berate the world, but to treat it with respect, even gentleness, all with the hope that in its own time, the world will join the Christians in glorifying God.[2]

Sermon Focus: Christian exiles turn away from their past behavior and their culture to follow the first exile, knowing that the one(s) rejected by society are God's chosen people.

Sermon Function: To reassure believers who are marginalized in their own society that Jesus was the first exile, and that in community with others they are chosen by God.

Sermon Sketch: *The First Exile*

To hold a set of convictions that are not shared by the majority culture inevitably results in self-doubt, often leading one either to retreat from the larger society or to assimilate into it. In our own time, the confession that Jesus Christ is Lord is offensive to a pluralistic society. Thus believers are tempted to doubt their own convictions. As Peter indicates, believers turn away from previous habits that were commonplace in their own society (2:1; cf. 1:14; 4:4), alienating their own society in the process. Apparently, this alienation led to an identity crisis, as it does for believers in a post-Christian society. Who are we? Can our convictions be true if they are widely rejected? Should we retreat in isolation like other minority groups?

1. But Peter invites us to come to Jesus, the first exile. He, too, was rejected by the world, but he was chosen and precious to God. If we are discouraged by our marginal status, we recall that Jesus was the first exile.

2. We do not come to the first exile alone, for we are together building the spiritual house. It is together that exiles realize that they are building blocks in God's temple. Exiles live in community with others.

3. Just as Jesus was rejected by the people of his time but accepted by God, we, too, are God's chosen people. We find our identity in him.

4. Therefore, we do not retreat from our society, but we declare the mighty acts of God, even evangelizing those who now reject our way of life. Evangelism, as 1 Peter indicates, happens when outsiders are attracted to the Christian lifestyle.[3]

2. Senior, *1 and 2 Peter*, 6–7.

3. See Stenschke, "Reading First Peter in the Context of Early Christian Mission," 117.

Chapter 2

RELATIONSHIPS BETWEEN
EXILES AND THE CULTURE

1 Peter 2:11—4:10

1 Peter 2:11–17. Exegetical Considerations. First Peter 2:11 marks a turning point in the letter, as the words "I appeal to you as strangers and exiles" indicate. One may compare Paul's transitions that begin with "I appeal to you" (*parakalō*, cf. Rom 12:1; Eph 4:1; Phil 4:2; 1 Thess 4:1). Only after Peter has given a breathtaking description of God's saving activity and the community's status as God's chosen people (1:1—2:10) does he describe the hard tasks of discipleship. Peter now begins a section that instructs believers about the exile existence in their particular station in life, addressing them once more as aliens and exiles. The introductory instruction to avoid fleshly desires that war against the soul (2:11) recalls the earlier warning about the desires (1:14). In this instance, however, Peter is introducing a section (2:13—3:7) that involves the exile's relationship to the institutions of society. In some instances, aliens and exiles withdraw from society's institutions while in other societies they draw the suspicion that they undermine the basic institutions of society. Peter indicates that some are calling the believers "evildoers" (2:12, 15).

The instructions address the believers' relationship to the basic institutions of society: the governing authorities (2:13–17), slavery (2:18–25), and marriage (3:1–7). Since the latter two instructions primarily address slaves and women, one may assume that the community includes primarily slaves and the women whose husbands were not believers (only one sentence is addressed to husbands). Peter does not advise the exiles to withdraw from society, but by "doing good" to have a positive influence and to silence those who accused them of undermining society's institutions.

Each instruction is introduced by a form of the verb "be subject" (*hypotassein*), a term formed by *hypo* (under) and *tassein* (order). According to Miroslav Volf,

> To be "subject" means to act in the freedom of the slaves of God (2:16) and, instead of provoking additional acts of violence, to curb violence by doing good (knowing all along that suffering will be one's lot because one cannot count on the victory of good over evil in this world). To be "subject" in a situation of conflict means to follow in the footsteps of the crucified Messiah and to refuse to take part in the automatism of revenge—"evil for evil or abuse for abuse" (3:9)—and to break the vicious circle of violence by suffering violence. If the injunction to be subject appears at first to function as a religious legitimation of oppression, it turns out, in fact, to be a *call to struggle against the politics of violence in the name of the politics of the crucified Messiah*. (emphasis Volf)[1]

Thus it means to accept one's place in an orderly arrangement (cf. 1 Cor 14:32, 34; 16:16; Eph 5:21). Christian existence involves not looking out for oneself but deferring to another. By accepting their place in the established order, believers reject the desire for power (cf. Eph 5:21), expressing themselves with humility in their relationships with others.

In the first instruction, "Be submissive to every human institution" (NRSV "accept the authority of every human institution"), Peter gives encouragement that was commonplace in early Christianity (cf. Rom 13:1–7; Titus 3:1). He is not giving a general theory about the Christian and the state but is addressing readers who are accused of undermining society. By submitting to the governing authorities, believers "silence the ignorance of foolish people" (2:15). Although these believers suffered as Christians, they did not engage in revolution or attempt to gain power. By submitting to the governing authorities, they demonstrated their concern for the public good. Although they are free in Christ, they do not use their freedom as the right to do evil. The imperatives in 2:17 demonstrate that believers do good deeds to both outsiders and insiders.

Merging the Horizons. While our communities do not share the general suspicion that they undermine the institutions of society, they are frequently

---

1. Volf, "Soft Difference," 22.

accused of advancing their own political influence at the expense of the public good. First Peter challenges believers to demonstrate their care for the communities in which they live. First Peter also indicates that submission and freedom are not opposed to each other. In our own society we face the constant conflict between the insistence on individual rights and the care for the common good. This conflict was most recently illustrated in the conflict over wearing masks in the midst of the pandemic.

Sermon Focus. Christian exiles do not withdraw from society but make a positive impression on others by contributing to the public good.

Sermon Function. To encourage listeners to "do good" and have a positive impact on the society.

Sermon Sketch: Freedom to Serve

According to the Declaration of Independence, we are endowed with "inalienable rights" to "life, liberty, and the pursuit of happiness." However, we have had the constant struggle over the relationship of individual rights to the well-being of society. Believers face that challenge also, for the Bible consistently declares that believers are free in Christ. But what does that mean in practice?

1. Like the believers in the first century, believers today face the suspicion that their primary interest is the securing of their own power and influence. In an increasingly secular age, churches fall under suspicion—sometimes deserved—that they seek only their own interests. First Peter indicates that believers are free but that they should be submissive to the institutions of society. Yes, submission is a good word. Christ elevated words such as submission and humility. Believers recognize more than their own interests.

2. Freedom is the freedom to do good. As Paul says, "Do good to all, especially those of the household of faith" (Gal 6:10). As believers, we pursue more than our own interests, for we look to the public good.

3. Looking out for the public good makes an impression on the world and silences the criticisms. It is a time to remember the lonely, to serve others, not to think about our own inconvenience. That is what believers have done in the past. In one famous example, the church historian Eusebius describes a fourth-century epidemic that swept through the Roman Empire. Eusebius records that far from fleeing the cities or

shutting off their homes from others, "all day long [Christians] tended to the dying and to the burial, countless numbers with no one to care for them. Others gather together from all parts of the city a multitude of those withered from famine and distributed bread to them all." As a result, Eusebius concludes, the Christians' "deeds were on everyone's lips, and they glorified the god of the Christians." (*Ecclesiastical History* 9.8)

1 Peter 2:18–25, 3:8–12. Exegetical Considerations. The advice to slaves (2:18–25) and wives (3:1–7) recalls the household codes of Eph 5:21—6:9 and Col 3:18—4:1. Unlike these household codes, however, 1 Peter offers no instructions to parents and children or masters, and it instructs husbands only briefly (3:7). Indeed, the submission of wives and slaves is commonplace in the New Testament and the surrounding culture (cf. Col 3:18; Eph 21–22; cf. Titus 2:9). While modern readers are undoubtedly dismayed by the appeal for submission of slaves and wives, these were the institutions of society over which Christians had no control. Furthermore, because Christians were being charged with rebellion against the institutions of society, submission signified that believers were not attempting to overcome the power structures. Thus submission took on a new meaning for Christians, for whom humility and deference to others was central to their moral discourse. The instruction to slaves to "suffer unjustly" (2:19) suggests that they are the models for all believers, who "suffer as Christians" (4:16; cf. 3:14) and do not "return evil for evil or abuse for abuse" (3:9).

The motivation for this countercultural view of submission is the Christian story, as Peter demonstrates in 2:21–25. Suffering abuse is not a misfortune but a calling (2:19), for it is the path of discipleship for believers. Just as Jesus was the first exile (2:4–10), he is the model for the community, for "he suffered for you, leaving an example, that you might walk in his steps." As in the advice to submit to governing authorities, Peter challenges the readers to "do good" (2:20; cf. 2:15), that is, to pursue the common good of everyone. In this instance, he motivates the listeners by an appeal to the Christian story of Jesus, the model of nonresistance.

In order to demonstrate that Christ is the model for those who "suffer as Christians" (4:16), this summary says "for Christ suffered for you" in 2:22 and 3:18 in contrast to other creedal statements that say "Christ died for our sins" (cf. 1 Cor 15:3).

The inclusion of the story of Jesus in the middle of the instructions to slaves is a reminder that the Christian lifestyle grows out of the Christian story. The words in 1 Pet 2:21–25 are so poetic that they may be known to the readers already. Without doubt these words were the center of the Christian proclamation that the believers heard when they were first converted. Their story shaped their character and their values. The passage is thus a reminder that all Christian morality is based on the Christian story of the One who did not seek his own power but left an example of submission for all who follow in his steps.

Like all societies, including our own, the people in the larger society had their own narrative that shaped their values. Peter offers a counter narrative for marginalized believers, indicating that the suffering of Jesus is the model for believers in all circumstances.

Merging the Horizons. Listeners will recognize that the horizon of this text could not possibly be further from our own time. The message to slaves evokes outrage and memories of the tragic experience in the United States. The preacher cannot avoid acknowledging this fact, even if a community of slaves in antiquity had no other options. Consequently, slavery is a reality also to Paul, who attempts to mitigate this reality by declaring that in Christ "there is no longer slave or free" (Gal 3:28) and instructing masters (e.g., Philemon) to receive the slave as a brother. In 1 Peter, however, there were apparently no masters. The challenge of slaves was to serve in the midst of the conditions in which they lived. Preachers see more in this text than the problem of slavery. It is a call to incorporate the Christian story in every circumstance in life.

While the worldview of most societies has been shaped by a controlling myth that shapes their values, the question in our society is whether it has any narrative that provides common values. Diversity is a value that we celebrate, but radical diversity can result in the loss of the unifying narrative that a society needs. The instructions to slaves indicate that the basic narrative shapes their response to their situation in life. What separates believers today is the narrative of the One who did not return evil for evil or look to his own interests.

Sermon Focus: The exile existence does not involve withdrawing from the world but in following the path of self-renunciation in all circumstances in life.

Sermon Function: To encourage listeners to walk in the steps and be shaped by the story of the One who submitted himself.

Sermon Sketch: *Knowing Our Story*

I confess that Peter's advice to slaves, like the numerous other passages in the New Testament, is disturbing, for slavery is repugnant. Ancient slavery was not comparable to slavery in our history, for the slavery had no association with racial background, and the slaves were often well educated and even tutors to the children. Nevertheless, it was an unfortunate reality in the ancient world, and Christian slaves had no options. First Peter addresses slaves of unbelieving masters—a difficult situation indeed.

I invite you to look beyond this reality to recognize that Peter addresses his readers where they are, challenging them to exhibit the behavior toward outsiders that will demonstrate that believers manifest discipleship wherever they are.

1. There is the call for submission, a word that makes us uncomfortable in a culture of individual rights. But submission meant looking out for the interests of others. In a world where slaves were accused of stealing (cf. Titus 2:9–10), Christian slaves, like all believers, do the good (2:20). This is the response that Peter gives to all believers in response to those who malign the community (1 Pet 2:15; 3:6).

2. But how do we define the good? No Christian teacher outlined a complete code of ethics or a list of activities that were suitable for each situation. Peter replies by recalling the Christian story: "Unto this you have been called, because Christ suffered for you, giving you an example, that you might follow in his steps." The answer was the Christian story that the believers heard when they were first converted. Jesus Christ was the submissive one, the one who did not retaliate. Exiles follow a path "in his steps."

3. Ancient people had their own narratives. Many held to the narrative that celebrated the individual's rise to power, celebrating heroes who claimed power for themselves. Modern people also have the narrative that shapes their values. However, as the sitcom *Seinfeld* (NBC, 1989–1998) demonstrated, many have no narrative, and thus few abiding values. Believers follow a countercultural narrative.

4. We are reminded of Paul's advice to the Philippians, who also lived in a culture that celebrated the rise to power. He told of the One who "was in the form of God" but "emptied himself," going to the cross.

5. While we do not have an exhaustive case law that defines Christian behavior, we have a story of the submissive One.

1 Peter 3:1–7. Exegetical Reflections. The instruction for wives to submit themselves to their own husbands is also the common expectation in antiquity and advice for wives elsewhere in the New Testament (Col 3:18; Eph 5:21–22). In this instance, Peter encourages wives to live by the common expectations of their culture. However, the instructions to wives are included in a series of exhortations involving the relationship of believers to outsiders. In a culture in which ancient moralists instructed wives to follow the religion of their husbands, the wives in 1 Peter have already violated societal expectations, placing them in a tenuous position. The slanders against Christians probably originated with husbands who were dismayed that their wives belonged to a strange cult. Thus Christianity divided families. The exhortation to submission belongs within the larger context of women who have apparently already displeased their husbands when they became Christians.

Although Christian wives have become believers without the consent of their husbands, their task is nevertheless to be submissive rather than engage in a power struggle. Peter offers a specific example of the good behavior of wives: they avoid the attire—braiding of hair, wearing of jewelry—that would offend the husband.

Good behavior toward outsiders has an evangelistic impact, as Peter indicates. Wives who defer to the husbands in demeanor may win the husbands to the faith. Peter had earlier said that those who saw good works among believers will "glorify God" when they see the good works (2:12). Exiles do not withdraw but make an impact on their society.

Merging the Horizons. In a culture of family breakdown, 1 Peter is a reminder that discipleship extends to commitments within the family. While the other household codes (Eph 5:21–22; Col 3:18—4:1) assume that both husbands and wives are believers, 1 Peter addresses a problem that was familiar both in antiquity and today: only one partner in the marriage is a believer. Thus 1 Peter reminds us that families come in all forms. Believers who follow the One who gave himself for others do not engage in a power struggle, as is often the case, but live in deference to the other's wishes. Peter speaks of the evangelistic witness of the woman who wins her husband by her selfless conduct. He is not addressing wives of abusive husbands but assumes that they live under normal conditions. Where both husbands and wives are believers (cf. 3:7), they are united in prayer. Thus discipleship extends to the family.

Sermon Focus: Discipleship in the home is a witness to nonbelievers.

Sermon Function: To encourage family members to recognize that discipleship extends to the home and family, where members look to the interests of others.

Sermon Sketch: *On Family Values*

1. "Be submissive to your own husbands," says Peter. The words make us uncomfortable in our egalitarian society. The words may evoke images of wives submitting to abusive husbands, or of cultures where wives are like property, or our negative reaction to the wedding vows where the wife is asked to promise that she will obey her husband. We no longer accept this picture of the domineering husband and the obedient wife. However, Peter is not suggesting that wives slavishly obey their husbands. In the Christian tradition, submission is not a bad word. In a world where wives were expected to adopt the religion of their husbands, the wives in 1 Peter have already disobeyed. Christianity has split families, and here the husband is a nonbeliever.

2. The suggestion that wives not adorn themselves with gold and costly clothing is also strange to us. But in antiquity, lavish dress by the wife was a form of rebellion against the husband. Thus submission means deferring to another. That is, discipleship occurs in the family when we look to the interests of the other.

3. Do you know what happens when we look to the interests of the other? Appropriate conduct is Christian witness. Few people have been argued into the faith, but they have been attracted to the Christian faith by the conduct of believers. Peter indicates that the wives might win over their hostile husbands. As a matter of fact, the growth of the early church took place when family members and neighbors recognized the moral conduct of believers. Believers acted graciously not only toward their own members but to their nonbelieving neighbors, and their families and friends noticed.

4. Indeed, in some instances, husbands and wives are partners in the faith. Believing husbands were not autocrats but lived with respect

toward their wives. As Peter says, "Show consideration for your wives." That is, they pray together; they are joint heirs of the grace of life.

5. Christian faith transforms family life. In a culture where the family is in crisis, believers are a counterculture of genuine family values and a witness to the world. The story of the One who gave himself for others affects every area of the believers' lives.

1 Peter 3:13–21. Exegetical Considerations. First Pet 3:13–21 continues the advice for how exiles interact with the surrounding culture, indicating the tenuous situation of believers. The *inclusio* in 3:13, 17 focuses on the importance of doing good for those who live in a hostile environment, continuing the theme that "doing good" will silence those who slander this exile community (cf. 2:12, 15, 16). As with the advice to slaves, Peter insists that only suffering for righteousness is beneficial (cf. 4:16). The exhortation "Do not fear what they fear," an allusion to the prophet's response to Israel's vulnerable situation (Isa 8:12), addresses the anxiety of people who have reason to fear as they suffer for righteousness's sake (3:14). The alternative to fear is to "sanctify God in [their] hearts" (3:15), as in Isaiah's time.

This confidence in God is the community's resource when believers are asked to give a reason for their hope. In this context the question comes from those who speak evil of them; thus it is a hostile or condescending question. To give a defense under these circumstances is a demonstration that one is not afraid of the hostile questioner but is able to articulate the reason for believing.

The term for defense is *apologia*, which is commonly used for a defense speech in a court of law (Acts 22:1; 2 Tim 4:18). In the second century those who defended the Christian faith to the wider public were the apologists. Their task was to give a reasoned defense of the faith before their detractors. Peter's advice, addressed to the entire community, indicates that all the listeners are capable of openly defending their faith in reasoned discourse.

Just as Christian slaves and wives respond to those who have authority with deference, believers answer those who ask hostile questions with "meekness and reverence" (3:16), choosing to suffer for "doing good" (3:17). Just as doing good will silence those who slander believers (2:15) and win nonbelieving husbands (3:1), it will "put to shame" those who ask hostile questions (3:16).

In 3:18–22 Peter offers the motivation for fearless engagement with the condescending question, as "because" in 3:18 indicates. The motivation, as in the advice to slaves, is once more the creedal statement. Believers suffer for doing good because "Christ suffered for sins." Unlike the previous creedal statement (2:21–25), however, this statement tells the entire story of Christ—his suffering, death, resurrection, and exaltation. That is, the suffering Christ ultimately triumphed. Christians may fearlessly articulate their faith to hostile listeners because they participate in the story of the One who ultimately triumphed after suffering.

Verses 19–21, which appear as a parenthesis in the creedal statement in verses 18–22, may be the most puzzling passage in the New Testament. These verses are a parenthesis between "made alive in the Spirit" (3:18) and "who has gone into heaven and is at the right hand of God, with angels, authorities, and powers made subject to him" (3:22). Between the resurrection (3:19) and exaltation (3:22) is the event when Christ "preached to the spirits in prison"—those who were disobedient in the time when Noah built the ark (3:20). The reference is probably an allusion to Jewish interpretations of the period such as the report in 1 Enoch that describes spirits in prison. The reference to the few who were saved "through the water" prefigures the experience of these believers, who are also few and have been saved by baptism, which has rescued them.

Preachers should not lose sight of the major point of the passage. Verses 18–22 indicate that suffering believers, few in number like the inhabitants of the ark, follow the suffering Christ, who was ultimately triumphant. They can defend their faith boldly to hostile questioners because they know that they will be vindicated. Just as the suffering Christ was triumphant, the suffering community has been saved and will be saved. In baptism, they have crossed from death to life.

Merging the Horizons. In a post-Christian culture, believers may not be confronted by overt persecution but by condescension and ridicule, intimidating believers from speaking freely. The exile community will flourish only when the whole community speaks boldly and when members are able to articulate their faith.

The sociologist Peter Berger was once asked, "Does Christianity have a future?" He answered that believers have been fascinated by the question, "What does modern man have to say to the church?" He concluded that it is time to ask, "What does the church have to say to modern man?" He added that ages of faith are marked by the proclamation of those who firmly believed that "they have grasped some important truths about the human condition."[2] He indicated that the strength of Christianity comes from its confidence in the power of its message.

Sermon Focus: We defend our faith boldly to a hostile listener, knowing our story of ultimate vindication.

Sermon Function: To embolden Christians in a post-Christian world to defend their faith and hope.

Sermon Sketch: Defenders of the Faith

"Let everyone be quick to listen, slow to speak," says the book of James (1:19). We can appreciate this wisdom because most of us wish at some point that we could retract words that we spoke in haste. However, there are also occasions when we didn't speak when we should have. We take an unpopular position, and we do not dare speak up. We have seen an injustice, but we did not speak. Fred Craddock told the story of his time at Vanderbilt in the 1960s. He went to his usual diner one evening, and only few were present. One was an African-American. He saw that the proprietor ignored the African-American, and he said nothing. When Craddock left, he said "I thought I heard the cock crow." He had failed to speak.

1. Undoubtedly, it is fear that prevents us from speaking up. In a post-Christian society, we may fear communicating convictions that are not popular. It was apparently that kind of fear that Peter had in mind when he said, "Do not fear what they fear; and do not be intimidated but sanctify Christ as Lord" (1 Pet 3:14).

2. It would have been easy to remain silent when hostile neighbors asked for a reason for their hope. But Peter challenges the listeners to "be ready to give a defense" to those who inquire. We, like the first readers, have received those inquiries. Sometimes they are condescending. At times their reason may be ridicule. But believers do not remain silent. Like a lawyer in the courtroom, they give a defense—Greek *apologia*—even when it is unpopular. Believers know how to articulate their faith.

3. Christianity undoubtedly survived because of those who gave a reasoned defense of their faith. The apologists of the second century addressed the leaders in times of persecution, defending their faith.

2. Berger, "Call for Authority in the Christian Community," 1261.

4. We do not have to live in fear; we can defend our faith openly because we believe the story of the one who died and triumphed over death (3:18–22). Peter recalls that only few were saved in the flood, suggesting that believers who stand firmly may also be few. But they can be fearless because of the One who triumphed after his suffering.

1 Peter 4:1–11. Exegetical Considerations. The opening words, "Since Christ suffered in the flesh," continue the theme of the suffering of Christ (cf. 2:21; 3:18) as the example for marginalized Christians who now suffer (2:19–20; 3:14; 4:16). Because Peter identifies the destiny of Jesus with the current situation of believers, he regularly indicates that Christ "suffered" rather than "Christ died" (cf. 1 Cor 15:3; 2 Cor 5:14). The identification of the suffering of Christ with the community is indicated in the imperative to the community: "Arm yourselves with the same mind" (4:1). The military metaphor is common in the New Testament (Rom 6:13; 13:12; 2 Cor 6:7; 10:4; Eph 6:10–17), suggesting that believers are engaged in a struggle in a hostile environment that requires rigorous preparation. Believers "arm themselves with the same intention" that Christ had, knowing that their suffering is the path of discipleship rather than a misfortune.

The imperative, "arm yourself," is the main focus of the passage, and the remainder of 4:1–11 offers support for this command, as "for" (*hoti*) in 4:1b indicates. That is, "the one who suffers—the believer—has ceased from sin." Suffering believers have made a major turn in their lives, which the rest of the passage describes. Suffering believers have turned away from the lifestyle in the practices shared by the surrounding culture ("the Gentiles")—licentiousness, passions, drunkenness, revelry. Indeed, their pagan neighbors are surprised at their behavior (4:4), and they respond with hostility. They, however, will face judgment, and the suffering believers will be vindicated (4:5–6).

As in 1 Pet 3:20–21, Peter refers mysteriously to an event that is otherwise unknown in Scripture but perhaps known to his audience. While scholars debate the meaning of the phrase, "preached to the dead," no one has satisfactorily explained the meaning, and it is useless to speculate. However, the larger point in 4:5–6 is that the oppressors will be judged and the oppressed will ultimately be vindicated.

If the believers have turned away from the vices of their own culture (4:2–6), they have turned toward conduct that unites the exiles in the community (4:7–11). One may observe the repetition of "one another." The exile existence is possible only in the context of the community. Believers love one another (4:8), express this love in hospitality for one another (4:9), use their gifts for one another (4:10–11), and unite in prayer.

Merging the Horizons. Few among us have made the radical change in our lifestyle that would lead our neighbors to be surprised that we no longer join them in "excesses of dissipation" (cf. 1 Pet 4:3–4). However, as the New Testament repeatedly indicates, conversion in the ancient world resulted in a radical change of lifestyle (cf. 1 Cor 6:9–11) and a rejection of the indulgence in sexual promiscuity and other vices. In the second century, Justin Martyr described the radical change that Christians had made in their pattern of life:

> Those who formerly delighted in fornication now embrace chastity alone; those who formerly made use of magical arts have dedicated themselves to the good and unbegotten God; we who once valued above everything the gaining of wealth and possessions now bring what we have into a common stock, and share with everyone in need; we who hated and destroyed one another, and would not share the same hearth with people of a different tribe on account of their different customs, now since the coming of Christ, live familiarly with them, and pray for our enemies. (*Apol.* 1.14)

This withdrawal from the immorality of society evoked the ridicule and hostility from the majority society. The situation in a post-Christian society is similar. Believers in a post-Christian society continue to value self-denial and chastity, separating themselves from their culture. Our task is not to restore Christian values into the public arena, restoring the Constantinian synthesis of Christ and culture but, as in Justin's time, to be a moral witness to the world by being a cohesive moral community, united as a family, practicing hospitality, and using our gifts for the sake of other Christian exiles.

Sermon Focus: Following Jesus in suffering involves turning away from the vices and values of our own culture, acquiring its hostility. However, knowing that they will be vindicated, exiles live together in a loving community.

Sermon Function: To urge the Christian exiles to continue in the loving practices that sustain the community, knowing that they will be vindicated.

Sermon Sketch: Arm Yourselves with the Same Mind

"Since therefore Christ suffered in the flesh, arm yourselves with the same intention," says Peter. He obviously had not read the books on church growth. I recall one group that canvassed the neighborhood, asking the people, "What would you like in a church?" Of course, we have a market-place of churches, and we have become comparison shoppers, looking for the benefits that each one offers. A church that conforms to the desires of the culture is scarcely a church of exiles.

1. "Arm yourselves?" This sounds like serious business. We are skittish about this military language. It sounds as if we may face hostile sur-roundings. Of course, we do not arm ourselves for offensive warfare. We arm ourselves with the mind of Christ. That is, we prepare our minds to live as exiles. We resist the hostile forces that would under-mine our faith.

2. We prepare our minds by resisting the allure of our culture's fascina-tion with sensual pleasures, the expressive individualism that focuses on individual freedom that commonly results in a new kind of slavery.

3. As we turn away from our culture and its values, we turn toward one another. Exiles survive and even flourish when they have the mutual support of others who share their commitments.

Chapter 3

SUFFERING AND VINDICATION

1 Peter 4:12—5:11

1 Peter 4:12–19. Exegetical Considerations. The theme of communal suffering continues in 4:12–19 as Peter encourages the community "not to be surprised at the fiery ordeal" that is happening as a test for them (4:12). The advice is reminiscent of Paul's reminder to the Thessalonians when they experienced hostility that "you yourselves know that this is what you are destined for" (1 Thess 3:3) and his word to the Philippians that it is a privilege to suffer, joining in the "same struggle" with him (Phil 1:28–29). That is, as Peter has insisted throughout the letter, one should not be surprised at "the fiery ordeal" because the Christian faith began with a suffering Savior and those who follow him will experience the same destiny.

The testing (*peirasmos*) by a fiery ordeal is reminiscent of the introductory words of 1 Peter, according to which the readers are "suffering various trials" (*peirasmoi*, also rendered as "tests") that test the genuineness of their faith, "being more precious than gold that, though perishable, is tested by fire" (1:6–7). The dramatic metaphor of the "fiery ordeal" is, of course the suffering that Peter addresses throughout the letter. Peter wants the discouraged community to see its suffering in perspective. It is a test that is to be expected.

The image of the test recalls the words of the Lord's Prayer, "Lead us not into temptation" (literally, test), and Paul's description of the church as a building that will be tested by fire (1 Cor 3:10–17). Jesus speaks of the seed that has no roots that withers away in a time of testing (Luke 8:13). In the garden Jesus says to Peter, "Stay awake and pray that you may not come into the time of trials; the spirit is willing, but the flesh is weak" (Matt 26:41). Testing is an inevitable part of Christian experience.

Testing is inevitable, but how do believers respond to the test? An extended period of testing may not be what believers expected. Many will undoubtedly be discouraged, if not defeated, by the test. Peter places the test in perspective (4:13–19) as the basis for the concluding imperative: believers must "entrust [themselves] to the faithful creator while continuing to do good" (4:19).

Having consistently indicated that believers follow the path of the suffering Christ (2:19–22; 3:18; 4:1), Peter now says that they share in the sufferings of Christ (4:15), experiencing abuse for the name of Christ (4:14). Believers can rejoice in anticipation of the ultimate rejoicing (4:13); indeed, it is a blessing (4:14; cf. 1:3–12). However, not all suffering is salutary, for some may suffer for doing evil. It is only when we suffer as Christians (4:16) that we have reason to rejoice.

Believers may rejoice when they recognize that their testing is not the end of their story, as 4:17–19 indicates. The "fiery ordeal" (4:12) that is taking place is God's judgment. Peter recalls the theme from the Old Testament, according to which God judges Israel before judging all the inhabitants of the earth (Jer 25:29). Suffering is the prelude to future glory for the faithful while the unfaithful will not escape. That is, suffering believers will be vindicated.

This passage provides assurance for a church that is "surprised" (4:12) by its current situation. Because they will survive God's judgment, they may now place themselves into the hands of the faithful creator, a moment of vindication.

Merging the Horizons. In some areas of the world, believers continue to face the "fiery ordeal" that tests their faith. In the Western world, believers continue to face tests of various kinds, and preachers will echo Peter's instruction "not to be surprised." The preacher may address believers who may be tested at the present, placing it in perspective. In the American context, many believers experience the test when their expectation of constant blessings faces the reality. Believers also face the test of marginalization in a society that is increasingly secular and dismissive of religious commitment.

Sermon Focus: Believers are inevitably tested by life's circumstances, especially in instances where they pay a price for their Christian commitment.

When they recall that they share in the sufferings of Christ, they can put their trust in God and anticipate future vindication.

Sermon Function: To reassure disillusioned believers who are disheartened when their faith is tested by circumstances.

Sermon Sketch: When Faith Is Tested

"Where is God?" was the response of the Jewish people who were trapped in the Warsaw ghetto. The same question is asked by all who have realized that bad things happen to those who have faith. Especially in churches in the West, we assume that religious faith brings peace and tranquility. But then we are surprised when bad things happen. Peter is more realistic; he tells a vulnerable audience, "Don't be surprised at the fiery ordeal." The "fiery ordeal" may come in many forms. And when it comes, our faith will be tested.

1. For the first believers, the testing was the "fiery ordeal" of marginalization and even persecution. Contrary to those who promise health and wealth for believers, every generation has its own test. Indeed, Jesus was tested before he began his mission. For some it is the discouragement over personal disappointment or tragedy. For others it is the test of apathy.

2. But how do we respond to the test? In Peter's words, "rejoice." As we recall in the opening words of the letter, written to exiles, "Blessed is the God and Father." Now he says that if you suffer for Christ's sake, you are blessed. We even rejoice in suffering, recognizing that we are sharing the sufferings of Christ. Yes, suffering of various sorts is inevitable, and we are not surprised. Indeed, we find joy in knowing that we share the destiny of all believers throughout history.

3. To experience a test is to recognize what lies in front of it. We are not defeated by the test but survive the test. We rejoice because God's ultimate judgment is our vindication.

1 Peter 5:1–7. Exegetical Considerations. Although Peter has said that each person has received a gift, including those of speaking and service (4:10–11), he now addresses elders (*presbyteroi*) and young people (*neōteroi*), just as he earlier addressed specific groups in the church, including slaves (2:18–25), wives (3:1–6), and husbands (3:7). Although *presbyteros* can refer either to a recognized office or to an older man; here it apparently refers to a recognized role within the church. Using a pastoral metaphor, he says that they "tend the flock," exercising oversight (*episkopountes*, 5:2). The metaphor of the shepherd is appropriate for the leader, for the Old Testament describes both God (Ps 23:1–4; Jer 13:17; 23:1–3) and human leaders (Isa 63:11; Jer 23:4) as shepherds. According to John's Gospel, Jesus is the good shepherd who gives his life for his sheep (John 10:11). What is meant by shepherding is in the verb *episkopountes* (NRSV "exercising oversight"; the noun form *episkopos* is usually rendered as *bishop* or *overseer*) and the antitheses that describe the temptations of the elders: "not for shameful gain . . . not under compulsion . . . not lording it over those in [their] charge." This is not a position of power, however, for the elders exemplify the countercultural lifestyle that is expected for all believers. Indeed, in the only first-person reference in the letter, Peter identifies with elders, calling himself a fellow elder and a witness to the sufferings of Christ (5:1), indicating that the elders are not exempt from suffering. The focus of the passage is the countercultural way that elders function. While leaders in the larger culture may use their positions "for sordid gain" (cf. Titus 1:7) or "lord it over" those under their authority, elders serve without compulsion and eagerly (5:2), and they do not "lord it over" those in their charge.

The rejection of the culture's competition for power is reminiscent of Jesus's statement to the disciples that "the kings of the earth lord it over them . . . , but not so with you; rather the greatest among you must become like the youngest, and the leader like one who serves" (Luke 22:24–25).

Those who devote themselves in suffering will receive the "crown of glory" that the chief shepherd will award (5:4). This is the Christian story. The Christ who humbled himself has triumphed over death. Those who humble themselves will be exalted.

Whereas the responsibility of those who are in authority is not to abuse their authority, the responsibility of those who are younger is to "submit to the elders" rather than rebel against authority. The reciprocal responsibilities of the elders/older people and the young people are reminiscent of the reciprocal responsibilities of husbands and wives. The exile community requires the harmony based on their countercultural existence. In a culture that places value on the exercise of power, the community follows the example of the One who suffered on their behalf.

Merging the Horizons. Responsible leaders are necessary for the exile community, and acknowledgement of their necessary function is indispensable also. For a culture in which individual rights and the exercise of power are paramount, the vision of leadership offered by 1 Peter is countercultural.

Leadership is not the exercise of power but the path of suffering and service, following the path of the suffering Christ and the leaders who have gone before us.

Sermon Focus: In the exile community, both the leaders and those who are led demonstrate the impact of the Christian story of humility and submission in the exercise of their discipleship.

Sermon Function: To encourage the community to practice attitudes toward leadership that are countercultural.

Sermon Sketch: *Leadership for Exiles*

We have seen enough instances of the failure of leadership that our society manifests a general distrust of all authority. We have seen so much abuse of power, incompetence, and financial mismanagement that we look with suspicion on any who wish to lead. Our cultural suspicion of leadership extends to the church. Indeed, news stories contain constant reminders of religious leaders who betray their trust. Yet, even exiles need leaders. While everyone has a gift and an area of service, we still need leaders, and leaders have responsibilities.

1. In the history of the church, Christian leadership has frequently mirrored secular power. As Jesus reminded his disciples, the leader is the one who serves. From ancient Corinth to our own time, the church has been tempted to adopt secular forms of leadership.

2. But Peter indicates a countercultural form of leadership. Following in the footsteps of Christ—and countless others through the centuries—leaders share in the afflictions of Christ. And Christian leaders do not abuse power, "lording it over" their members. They are like shepherds looking out after the flock.

3. It is not only Christian leaders who follow in the footsteps of the one who sacrificed for others, but all others follow the path of humility, submitting to those who lead. Peter's advice to "young people" is actually a word for all who are not in positions of authority. Our understanding of leadership is defined by humility (5:5–6).

1 Peter 5:8–11. Exegetical Considerations. Final words are no less important for a communication than the opening words. Orators spoke of the peroration that summarized the message with added intensity. 1 Peter reaches the conclusion with a final word of encouragement in the context of suffering. In these final words a series of imperatives (5:6–9) indicating the communal response to its situation is sandwiched between two passages that reassure the community of faithfulness to them (5:6–8, 10–11).

Peter concludes the letter with two dimensions of the community's response. In the first place, after encouraging the listeners to humble themselves toward one another (5:5), Peter now encourages them to humble themselves before God (5:6) as they "throw their anxieties before God" (5:7), knowing that God cares for them. Already he has said, "Let those who suffer according to God's will do right and entrust their souls to a faithful Creator" (4:19). These are the anxieties of the vulnerable house church. This is reminiscent of the earlier exhortations for the vulnerable community not to fear hostile forces (3:14) but to fear God (cf. 1:17; 2:18; 3:16). Christians have already experienced the fidelity and the love of God. They know that God cares because they have been "born again" into God's new world. They are the beneficiaries of blessings that were inaccessible even to the prophets (1:10–12)! Whenever anxiety lurks over them, they need only to recall the signs that "God cares for them." Jesus's words about anxiety are accompanied by his reminder that the God who clothes the lilies of the field will also take care of his children (Matt 6:25–33).

In the second place, he encourages the listeners to "discipline" themselves, "keep alert" (5:8), and "resist" (5:9). While the opposition in earlier parts of the letter is the surrounding society, here the opposition is from "your adversary, the devil," who prowls around "like a roaring lion" (5:8). New Testament writers consistently point to the threats posed by the devil. From the temptation of Jesus (Matt 4:1–11) to the frequent warnings in the New Testament (cf. Eph 4:27; 6:11; 1 Tim 3:6; Jas 4:7), the adversary is a constant danger for believers. Despite the danger posed by the devil, believers who face threats to their existence know of the God who cares for them. Thus having assured the readers of God's care, Peter urges the community's resistance, knowing that they belong to a worldwide family that is also suffering. Indeed, the greetings from the church in "Babylon"—apparently Rome—is a reminder that the local house church belongs to a worldwide movement.

Believers can resist because their suffering is not the end of the story. After they have suffered for a little while, the God of all grace will "restore, support, strengthen, and establish" them (5:11). Thus Peter places suffering in perspective, indicating that it is temporary and that ultimately their suffering will cease and God will triumph. This letter, addressed to a suffering community, ends as it began: with praise to God (5:11). A letter addressed to a marginalized community ends in a doxology (5:12).

Merging the Horizons. While the ancient readers recognized the dangers to the church in a hostile society, believers now are called upon to resist the current dangers. Modern readers, especially in the West, may not identify with the suffering of the original readers. Discussion of the adversary, the devil, is especially foreign to contemporary Christians. However, as Peter indicates, the devil appears in concrete form in the community's hostile neighbors and the temptations that face the church. Believers still face their own anxieties and temptations, and they face the "roaring lion" in various forms. Believers are always tempted to adapt to the dominant culture, and they face the anxiety of living in a post-Christian society. The call to resist, trusting in God's sovereign control, is relevant for the church in all societies.

Sermon Focus: The church acknowledges real dangers, but stands firm and resists evil, knowing that God will ultimately triumph.

Sermon Function: To acknowledge the danger facing the church and reassure the listeners of God's care.

Sermon Sketch: *Danger and Reassurance*

The devil disappeared from our discourse long ago. Indeed, we may be uncomfortable with the reference in 1 Peter to the devil who is like a lion prowling around and seeking to devour us. To the modern reader this language appears antiquated. We do not speak much of "your adversary, the devil." In the context of a Christianity that demands little, we seldom think of the Christian faith as a battle against a formidable adversary. Who comes here to the pleasant surroundings of the modern church conscious of a roaring lion who is out to devour us? And who comes thinking that the world is our enemy and we are the prey? I doubt if anyone comes expecting to hear that blood-curdling roar. We are reminded of those awful images of the devil that we have seen in popular parlance.

1. But, as Peter reminds us, the devil comes in many forms. For him, the hostility facing the church was the "roaring lion." This was an image for the danger facing the church and its feeling of powerlessness against various forces. In the words of the classic hymn "The Church's One Foundation," the church has always been "by schism

rent asunder, by heresies distressed." There is a roaring lion, and the church feels powerless.

2. The church lives with anxiety. But as Peter encourages us, we "cast our anxieties" on the One who cares for us. The church lives in the conviction that God cares for the people of faith. We are not powerless.

3. Because God cares for us, we do not run and hide. We stand. We resist, knowing that we place ourselves in the hands of God.

BIBLIOGRAPHY

Achtemeier, Paul. *1 Peter*. Hermeneia. Minneapolis: Fortress, 1996.

Attridge, Harold W. *The Epistle to the Hebrews: A Commentary on the Epistle to the Hebrews*. Hermeneia. Philadelphia: Fortress, 1989.

Berger, Peter. "A Call for Authority in the Christian Community." *Christian Century* (September 27, 1971), 1257–63.

Bruce, F. F. *The Epistle to the Hebrews*. Grand Rapids: Eerdmans, 1990.

Buttrick, David. *Homiletic: Moves and Structures*. Minneapolis: Fortress, 1987.

Buechner, Frederick. *Telling the Truth: The Gospel as Comedy, Tragedy, Fairy Tale*. New York: Harper, 1977.

Craddock, Fred B. *As One without Authority*. St. Louis: Chalice, 2001.

———. *Preaching*. Nashville: Abingdon, 1985.

Davids, Peter. *The First Epistle of Peter*. New International Commentary on the New Testament. Grand Rapids: Eerdmans, 1990.

deSilva, David A. *Perseverance in Gratitude: A Socio-Rhetorical Commentary on the "Epistle to the Hebrews."* Grand Rapids: Eerdmans, 2000.

Ellingworth, Paul. *The Epistle to the Hebrews: A Commentary on the Greek Text*. Grand Rapids: Eerdmans, 1993.

Elliott, John H. *A Home for the Homeless: A Sociological Exegesis of 1 Peter, Its Situation and Strategy*. Philadelphia: Fortress, 1981.

———. *1 Peter: A New Translation with Introduction and Commentary*. AB 37B. New York: Doubleday, 2000.

Feldmeier, Reinhard. *Die Christen als Fremde: Die Metapher der Fremde in der antiken Welt, im Urchristentum und im 1. Petrusbrief*. Tübingen: J. C. B. Mohr, 1992.

———. *The First Letter of Peter. A Commentary on the Greek Text*. Translated by Peter Davids. Waco, TX: Baylor University Press, 2008.

Gupta, Nijay. *Paul and the Language of Faith*. Grand Rapids: Eerdmans, 2020.

Johnson, Luke Timothy. *Hebrews: A Commentary*. New Testament Library. Louisville: Westminster John Knox, 2012.

Jones, L. Gregory. "Formed and Transformed by Scripture: Character, Community, and Authority in Biblical Interpretation." In *Character and Scripture: Moral Formation, Community, and Biblical Interpretation*, edited by William P. Brown, 16–33. Grand Rapids: Eerdmans, 2002.

Lane, William L. *Hebrews 1–8*. Word Biblical Commentary. Dallas: Word, 1991.

———. *Hebrews 9–13*. Word Biblical Commentary. Dallas: Word, 1991.

Long, Thomas. *Hebrews*, Interpretation, a Bible Commentary for Teaching and Preaching. Louisville: Westminster John Knox, 1997.

———. *The Witness of Preaching*. 3rd ed. Louisville: Westminster John Knox, 2016.

Martin, J. Ramsey. *1 Peter*. Word Biblical Commentary. Waco, TX: Word, 1988.

Macbride, Tim, "Preaching to Aliens and Strangers: Preaching the New Testament as Minority Group Rhetoric." *The Journal of the Evangelical Homiletics Society* 16 (2016): 6–15.

Mitchell, Alan C. *Hebrews*, Sacra Pagina 13. Collegeville, MN: Liturgical, 2007.

Niemoller, Martin. *Exile in the Fatherland*. Grand Rapids: Eerdmans, 1986.

Schnelle, Udo. *The First Hundred Years of Christianity*. Translated by James W. Thompson. Grand Rapids: Baker Academic, 2020.

Senior, Donald P. *1–2 Peter*. New Testament Message: a Biblical-Theological Commentary. Wilmington: Michael Glazier, 1980.

———. *1 Peter, Jude, and 2 Peter*. Sacra Pagina 15. Collegeville, MN: Liturgical Press, 2003.

Smith, Shively T. J. *Strangers to Family: Diaspora and 1 Peter's Invention of God's Household*. Waco, TX: Baylor University Press, 2016.

Stenschke, Christoph. "Reading First Peter in the Context of Early Christian Mission." *Tyndale Bulletin* (2009): 107–26.

Thompson, James W. *Hebrews*. Paideia. Grand Rapids: Baker Academic, 2008.

Volf, Miroslav. "Soft Difference: Theological Reflections on the Relation between Church and Culture in 1 Peter." *Ex Auditu* 10 (1994): 15–30.

Willimon, William. *The Gospel for the Person Who Has Everything*. Valley Forge: Judson, 1978.